THE
GREAT IRISH
TENOR

THE GREAT IRISH TENOR

Gordon T. Ledbetter

CHARLES SCRIBNER'S SONS

NEW YORK

1 3 5 7 9 11 13 15 17 19 I/C 20 18 16 14 12 10 8 6 4 2

Printed in Great Britain
Library of Congress Catalog Card Number 77-84381
ISBN 0-684-15517-6

CONTENTS

FOREWORD

I am indebted to my sister, Audrey Baker, for her many suggestions and ideas during the writing of this book, and for her great patience; to Liam Breen for putting his entire collection of memorabilia at my disposal and for many kindnesses; to Sorcha Cusack, who provided me with many newsclips and with much encouragement; and to Cyril, Count McCormack, who graciously answered my many questions. I am grateful to many people who supplied me with information and pictures, especially Dr J. P. Cavarai, Ernie Bayly, the editor of the *Talking Machine International*, Peter Dolan, Billy English, Professor E. Forti, Perceval Graves, Denis Hayden, the late Josie Hoyle, Seamus Kearns, Joe Linnane, Eddie O'Connor, Seamus O'Dwyer, Robert Duke Williams; and Robert L. Webster, for providing me not only with many pictures but with access to his fine collection of McCormack records. I have Angela Milburn to thank for much editorial assistance.

I am grateful to W. H. Allen & Co. Ltd for permission to quote from Lily McCormack's *I Hear You Calling Me*; and to Bing Crosby and Curtis Brown Ltd who have allowed me to quote from *Call Me Lucky*, published by F. Muller Ltd. I have Joseph Murrells and Barrie & Jenkins to thank for the use of an extract from *The Book of Golden Discs*. Henry Pleasants and John Farquharson Ltd have kindly given me permission to quote from *The Great Singers from the dawn of opera to our own time*, and *Serious Music and All That Jazz*, both published by V. Gollancz Ltd, and to Henry Pleasants I am indebted for enlightening conversations. I am grateful to G. P. Putnam's Sons for the use of material from C. L. Wagner's *Seeing Stars*, to Harold Rosenthal and Putnam for an extract from *Two Centuries of Opera at Covent Garden*; and to J. B. Steane and G. Duckworth & Co. Ltd for permission to quote from *The Grand Tradition*. Robert Duke Williams has generously allowed me to quote from the unpublished memoirs of Alexander Williams RHA.

I acknowledge my thanks to the following publications for permission to use quoted extracts and visual material: *The Boston Sunday Post, Daily Telegraph, Gramophone,* Grove's *Dictionary of Music and Musicians, Hi-Fidelity Magazine, Illustrated London News, The Irish Times, The Irish Independent, King Features, Il Mattino, Melbourne Herald, Musical America, New York Herald, New York Times, Punch, Sunday Times, The Record Collector* and *The Times.* I am most grateful to the following organizations and institutions for their help: The British Museum, The Library of Congress, The Italian Cultural Institute in Dublin, The National Library of Ireland, The New York Public Library, The McCormack Societies of America, Greater Kansas City Inc. and of Ireland, the Archives of the Royal Opera, Covent Garden, The Trinity College Library (especially to Liz Gleeson, Sheila NíThiarnaigh, Harry Bouvenizer and Jim O'Keefe for their unfailing help), to the Radio Times Hulton Picture Library and to the United States Department of the Interior, National Park Service, Edison National Historic Site.

Finally, I should like to express my gratitude to Dr Tom Walsh of Wexford, for reading the manuscript during its preparation and for making many useful suggestions.

Wicklow
January 1977

Gordon T. Ledbetter

An Edison Standard Phonograph with a leather and tin collapsible horn. This is the type most frequently met with today. It appeared in seven models, the first of which was introduced in 1898, and the cost was then $20 or £4. The example pictured above is of the Standard Phonograph Model D, introduced in the United States in 1908 and in Britain the following year. It incorporated a gear-change device attached to the feed screw, so that both two and four minute cylinders could be played. Four minute cylinders contained two hundred grooves to the inch – twice as many as the two minute cylinders. Thus, for playing four minute cylinders the feed screw was required to revolve at half the speed required for two minute ones. Initially, the purchaser had the option of a brass horn or hearing tubes. The leather horn shown folded, right, would have been bought subsequently.

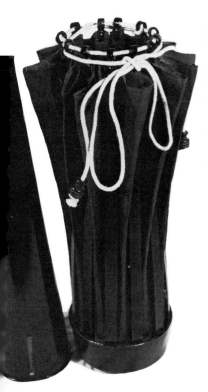

Prelude

THE TALKING MACHINE

Suddenly, and with less than forty years between them, the photographic camera and the cylinder phonograph made their appearance. The interval was certainly short. Before the arrival of these two inventions, the latest means of documenting the present came with the systematic writing of language. And that development took place an estimated five thousand years earlier.

When Louis Jacques Mandé Daguerre (1787–1851) announced his process of photography in Paris in 1839, France, Europe and indeed the whole world responded immediately. Professional photographers sprang up in virtually every capital city, and everyone who could afford it flocked to have their likeness taken. Photography was an instant success. When in 1877, in New Jersey, USA, Thomas Alva Edison (1847–1931) devised a machine that could record and reproduce sound, the world reacted with amazement – and then quickly forgot about it.

It is curious how differently the two inventions were received. The reason probably had much to do with the fact that the first photographs were extremely life-like whereas the first cylinder recordings were not. The immediate impact of photography perhaps also stemmed from its appeal to vanity, although it has to be admitted that this was not always the spirit in which it was received. When Queen Victoria asked her court painter, the Frenchman Alfred Chalfont, if he did not think photography would make painting redundant, he is said to have replied, 'Ah non, Madame! Photographie can't flattère.' Perhaps sound recording was found to be even less flattering. Certainly few who hear their voices played back for the first time relish the experience; and a speech recording is arguably more revealing than a photograph. When Columbia, disingenuously, advertised that one of the advantages of the phonograph was that 'Poor writers and spellers are enabled to

The original tin-foil phonograph of ?
This model was sent to England ?
Edison applied for a British patent. In ?
it was transferred from the Patent Mus?
to the Science Museum in South Kens?
ton, London. On the fiftieth anniversa?
its invention, it was returned to Ediso?
his request. It is now in the E?
Museum, West Orange, New Jersey.

communicate by mail without disclosure of their educational defects', the company could hardly have been further from the truth. In our physical appearance, the way we dress and part our hair, as in the way we write, we constantly cross barriers of class, but rarely is our speech so obliging.

Fired by the photographic perception of Juliet Margaret Cameron, the art critic Roger Fry (1866–1934) expressed the hope that:

> One day . . . the National Portrait Gallery will be deprived of so large a part of its grant that it will turn to fostering the art of photography and will rely on its results for its records instead of buying acres of canvas covered at great expense by fashionable practitioners in paint.

Whatever the respective merits of painting and photography (and their functions) these media are to a degree interchangeable. There has never been an alternative to sound recording. Visual representation of history goes back as far as cave and wall paintings and primitive sculptures. Aural history of the same is no older than the phonograph. Had the period following its inception in 1877 been used for the development of sound recording, we might now be able to listen to, among so many others, the voice of Jenny Lind (1820–87) and the piano of Franz Liszt (1811–86). Indeed we might have had aural history stretching much further back. For so simple the construction, so readily available the materials required for a phonograph, that the event of sound recording and reproduction, unlike photography, could have taken place two thousand years ago.

Close-up of an Edison Model C stylus.

Edison's phonograph consisted essentially of a revolving cylinder of tin foil, later of wax, which also moved laterally on account of a thread screw along its axle. Sound vibrations received by a diaphragm were transferred to a recording stylus. The stylus then embedded a helical series of indentations on the tin foil. On running a second, smoother, stylus over the indentations the original vibrations were again set up on the diaphragm and thence transmitted into the surrounding air. The most advanced element in the design of the phonograph was the thread or feed screw. Used in conjunction with a worm, the most common arrangement was for the screw to drive the stylus along the length of the cylinder during the process of cutting the groove and during playback. Less frequently, it was the cylinder that travelled lengthwise while rotating and the stylus remained in a fixed position. Occasionally some phonographs, notably the German Puck machines, were marketed which dispensed with a feed screw altogether. As with the disc gramophone, the styli of these machines depended upon the walls of the groove for guidance. This, of course, was feasible only where playback was concerned and the groove had already been cut during recording.

The worm screw is an advance on Archimedes' screw, which was said to have been used in the third century BC for removing water from a ship's hold. So the phonograph as Edison conceived it could not have pre-dated Archimedes, who lived *c.* 287–212 BC. But a spiral groove is not an absolute necessity. A recording, albeit of very limited duration, could be made not only on the length of a cylinder but also on the edge of a wheel and consisting of but a single revolution. The potter's wheel could have served that purpose. If such means are allowed, then the period in which man might first have constructed a primitive phonograph or gramophone goes so far back as to be indeterminate. (I shall follow European usage in speaking of phonograph and gramophone when referring, respectively, to cylinder and disc machines.)

Certain it is that the actual construction of a talking machine would have offered the Ancients little trouble. What they could not do, for all their ingenuity, was to make the imaginative leap to envisage sound vibrations as a source of physical indentations and physical indentations as a source of sound. That realization came slowly, and when it came there was more than one man working along similar lines. Edison was the first to reproduce sound waves but he was not the first to conceive a means of doing so, and he was not the first to *record* sound waves. This event had taken place twenty years earlier, in 1857, on a machine called a phonautograph, the brainchild of Edouard Leon Scott de Martinville (1817–79). His machine consisted of a cylinder coated with lampblack, a diaphragm and a hog's bristle for a stylus. When the diaphragm was subjected to sound vibrations the bristle traced a wavy line through the lampblack. By such means, Scott was able to demonstrate that a correlation existed between the character of the wavy line and the kind of sounds received by the diaphragm. In a word, the wavy line was a sound-track.

Then on 10 April 1877, Charles Cros (1842–88), a poet and scientist, registered with the Académie des Sciences in Paris a method of photo-engraving the sound-track produced on a lampblacked surface so as to obtain a three-dimensional, permanent, groove. This groove, he argued, could then become the means of reproducing the sounds that had originally created the wavy line. His theory was, essentially, valid. So Cros may be said to have been the first man to conceive a viable method of sound recording and reproduction. But he failed in his attempts to put the theory into practice.

Eight months later Edison succeeded, apparently without any knowledge of his predecessors. The source of his inspiration had come mainly from his familiarity with telegraphy, invented by Morse in 1844, and the telephone, invented by Gray and Bell in 1876. The deafness from which he suffered made Edison attach a sharp point to a telephone diaphragm in order to increase its volume, and the vibrations of the diaphragm actually caused the point to prick his finger. The phenomenon became the basis for his telephonic repeater, which consisted of a diaphragm and embossing point which recorded morse code on a rotating disc of paraffin paper, or a laterally moving strip of the same material. In the course of experimenting with this device, Edison

Charles Cros

...dison examining a reproducer – the stylus ...d diaphragm assembly. Originally, the ...roducer was known under the less ...phisticated title of 'speaker'.

thought he could hear the indistinct reproduction of his own shouted 'hullo', and even of music. On a laboratory work sheet dated 18 July 1877, which noted these experiments, Edison asserted that, 'there is no doubt that I shall be able to store up and reproduce automatically at any future time the human voice perfectly.' Such was his confidence in this idea that Edison allowed his assitant Edward H. Johnson to make it public through a letter published in the *Scientific American* on 17 November. Johnson's letter ended: 'In view of the practical inventions already contributed by Mr Edison, is there anyone who is prepared to gainsay this prediction? I for one am satisfied it will be fulfilled, and that, too, at an early date.'

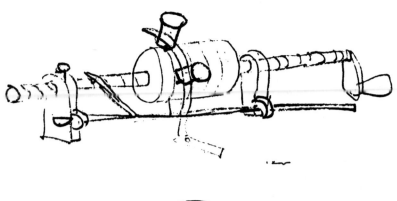

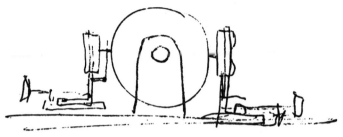

The two sketches Edison prepared fo workman, John Kreusi, and from u was constructed the first tin-foil ph graph. The sketches are dated 29 Nover 1877.

The date was 6 December 1877. In front of a sceptical workman, John Kreusi, who had just completed the machine, Edison shouted into the mouthpiece the words 'Mary had a little lamb . . .', and moments later, through the tortuous sound of tin foil under stress, heard his voice played back. On 22 December the *Scientific American* reported that:

> Mr Thomas Edison recently came into this office, placed a little machine on our desk, turned a crank and the machine enquired as to our health, asked how we like the phonograph, informed us that *it* was very well, and bid us a cordial good-night. These remarks were not only perfectly audible to ourselves, but to a dozen or more persons gathered around . . .

The same article proceeded to express wonder and surprise at the powers of modern machinery, particularly at this very small piece, not much bigger than the contemporary camera, which was able to produce words of human speech; unclear and barely audible they might be, but yet undoubtedly human and therefore all the more weird. The article finished by foretelling:

> When it becomes possible, as it doubtless will, to magnify the sound, the voices of such singers as Parepa and Tietiens will not die with them, but will remain as long as the metal in which they may be embodied will last.

Edison became a celebrity. In April 1878 he travelled to the White House to demonstrate his invention, and Rutherford B. Hayes became

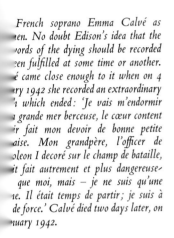

French soprano Emma Calvé as ...en. No doubt Edison's idea that the ...ords of the dying should be recorded ...en fulfilled at some time or another. ...é came close enough to it when on 4 ...ry 1942 she recorded an extraordinary ...h which ended: 'Je vais m'endormir ...a grande mer berceuse, le cœur content ...r fait mon devoir de bonne petite ...aise. Mon grandpère, l'officer de ...oleon I decoré sur le champ de bataille, ...t fait autrement et plus dangereuse ...que moi, mais — je ne suis qu'une ...e. Il était temps de partir; je suis à ...de force.' Calvé died two days later, on ...nuary 1942.

the first president to record. Unfortunately, the cylinders have been lost.

It is sometimes thought that Edison was not aware of the potential of his invention, but this was far from being the case. When he patented his talking machine he envisaged it being used for:

> Letter writing and all kinds of dictations; phonographic books; the teaching of elocution; talking clocks that should announce in articulate speech the time for going home, going to meals etc., a Registry of Sayings, Reminiscences etc. by members of a family in their own voices, and the last words of dying persons.

The value of recording to industry is now taken for granted though not, perhaps, for its ability to 'announce in articulate speech the time for going home'. Nevertheless, talking clocks did have a vogue as a substitute for chiming bells and cuckoo calls. One German company, B. Hiller, manufactured no less than three hundred talking clocks built to their 1911 model specifications. And it was rarely short of words, announcing the time, as it did, every quarter of an hour for twelve hours a day. Although families recorded conversations for their own amusement, a register of sayings by members of a family never enjoyed the same vogue as the hallowed family photographic album did before the First World War. But only one of Edison's ideas failed to have any vogue at all. That was the idea of recording 'the last words of the dying'. Maybe the phonograph arrived too late. But whatever our dismay at the Victorian preoccupation with the death-bed, it could not be greater than would be theirs at our preoccupation with the mating one.

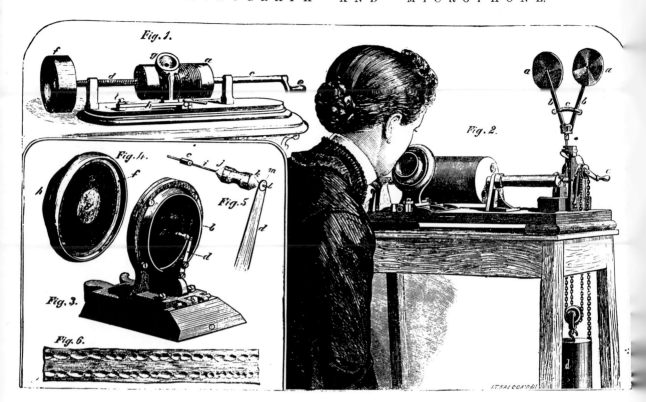

On 3 August 1878 the *Illustrated London News* devoted three columns of writing and a page of drawings to the wonderful talking machine. The article began, 'This is an age of scientific marvels, if not of miracles . . .' and went on rather unscientifically:

> Witnessing its performances, one is apt to take the stories of genii bottled up for long years to be freed at last, of frozen tunes, released by warmth, flooding the air with melody, and other romances of a like kind, as veritable prophecies of the good time coming, couched in this sort of rollicking nonsense to hide their true meaning from the uninitiated, and possibly to save the narrators' heads.

But the good time was not yet at hand. Edison left his invention untouched for almost ten years. In the interval, he produced the first incandescent lamp – made of carbonized cotton – which blazed, uninterrupted, for forty hours.

Meanwhile, Alexander Bell (1847–1922), with the prize money of $10,000 which he had won for the invention of the telephone, had set up his Volta Laboratory in Washington D.C. He was joined by his cousin Chichester Bell (1848–1924) and Charles S. Tainter (1854–1940). They experimented along the lines of Edison's tin-foil phonograph and

Drawings of the phonograph from Illustrated London News, *3 Au[g] 1878. Fig. 1 shows a phonograph mod[el] from the original tin-foil model by [the] addition of a heavy fly-wheel 'to secure [as] far as possible uniformity of motion'. [This] was the design Edison demonstrated at [the] White House in April 1878. The [two] brass discs in Fig. 2 also acted as a gover[nor]. Note the weight suspended by a ch[ain] underneath the table and connected t[o a] pulley at the axle of the cylinder. As [the] weight descended – so rotating the cylinde[r] – it was possible to wind up the chain, a[nd] maintain the motion of the cylinder with[out] interruption. Figs. 3 and 5 show [the] reproducer, and Fig. 6 the indentations o[f the] sound track.*

produced their own machine. But more significantly, they dispensed with Edison's tin foil as a medium of recording and used cardboard cylinders coated with paraffin wax instead. This made a very substantial reduction in surface noise. In 1887 The Graphophone Company, later re-named Columbia, was formed for the production of dictating machines.

Seeing his rivals exploiting his invention, Edison came back sharply on the scene. From the beginning, he had envisaged the possibility of using wax as a medium of recording. In May 1888 he received a patent for a solid wax cylinder, and in the same month he produced his Improved Edison Phonograph. This he immediately followed with The Perfected Edison Phonograph. But the first commercial years of sound recording were disappointing. There were mechanical difficulties and another wonder of the age, the electric motor, proved unsatisfactory. In 1893 the Greenhill Mechanical Phonograph Motor was announced, and *The Phonogram*, a monthly journal 'devoted to the science of sound' sang its praises while announcing that 'few persons will [now] be troubled with electricity. It will be absurd to attempt to force a troublesome method of driving power upon the public.'

Dictating machines were not regarded as a necessity by business houses, as they are today, and the early phonograph required something

...ison advertisement 'Looking for the ...d'. One of the most charming of early ...onograph advertisements, perhaps be-...se the theme is universal to childhood.

THE EDISON PHONOGRAPH

THE ACME OF REALISM.

EVERY GENUINE EDISON PHONOGRAPH BEARS THIS

TRADE

Thomas A Edison

MARK.

"LOOKING FOR THE BAND"

of a knack to operate. Moreover, stenographers were not overjoyed with the prospect of redundancy and formed a lively opposition. This current advertisement was unlikely to flatter their sensibilities:

> Ten reasons why Edison's phonograph is superior to any stenographer. One: Speed – You can dictate as rapidly as you please, and are never asked to repeat. Two: Convenience – You dictate alone, at any hour of day or night. Three: Saving of Operator's Time – During dictation operator can be employed with other work. Four: Accuracy – The Phonograph can only repeat what has been said to it . . . Eight: Tirelessness – The Phonograph needs no vacation. Does not grumble at any amount of overwork . . .

In England, publicity for Edison's phonograph was in the hands of a certain Colonel Gouraud. He wrote a letter to *The Times*, 26 June 1888:

> Sir – At two o'clock this afternoon, at the address below, I had the honour to receive from Mr Edison his 'Perfected Phonograph' . . . At five minutes past two o'clock precisely, I and my family were enjoying the at once unprecedented and astounding experience of listening to Mr Edison's own familiar and unmistakable tones here in England – more than 3,000 miles from the place where he had spoken and exactly ten days after, the voice meanwhile having voyaged across the Atlantic Ocean . . .

Colonel Gouraud continued the letter in a vein of high enthusiasm: Edison was to send him letters in the form of dictated messages recorded on phonograms (or cylinders) and Gouraud was to reply in the same manner, Edison having remarked that he would find Gouraud's dictated letters easier to understand than those written in illegible handwriting. Gouraud also described the musical recordings that he had received from Edison, who claimed to have played them innumerable times; this was probably an exaggeration for the purposes of advertisement, since wax cylinders wore out fairly fast. Gouraud concluded with the same optimism with which he had begun:

> Altogether our experiences of the day have been so delightful and unusual, not to say supernatural, that it makes it difficult to realize that we have not been dreaming . . .
>
> I have the honour to be, Sir, your obedient servant,
>
> G. E. Gouraud,
>
> LITTLE MENLO, BEULAH-HILL, UPPER NORWOOD, SURREY.

P.S. It may be interesting to add that the above communication was spoken by me into the phonograph and written from the

On the front page of the Illustrated London News, 14 July 1888, the upper drawing shows the Press Gallery at the Crystal Palace during the Handel Festival with '. . . the phonograph reporting with perfect accuracy the sublime strains, vocal and instrumental, of the "Israel in Egypt" received by a large horn projecting over the balustrade. The "phonograms" being sent to Mr Edison, all the Handel choruses, as sung here by four thousand voices, with the orchestral and organ accompaniments, will be heard in New York and in other American cities. They can be repeated to a hundred different audiences for years to come.' Note the cumbersome wet-cell batteries under the table. The lower picture is of Colonel Gouraud surrounded by his family, listening to the phonograms Edison had despatched to him from New York.

THE ILLUSTRATED LONDON NEWS

REGISTERED AT THE GENERAL POST-OFFICE FOR TRANSMISSION ABROAD.

No. 2569.-- VOL. XCIII. SATURDAY, JULY 14, 1888. SIXPENCE.
By Post, 6½d.

phonograph's dictation by a member of my family, who had, of course, no previous experience of the instrument.

Gouraud then invited the great and the glorified to record messages of congratulation to Edison. Many of these cylinders were later exhibited at the Crystal Palace. Those who accepted the invitation included Oscar Wilde, Robert Browning, and Sir Arthur Sullivan who prophecied:

> For myself I can only say that I am astonished and somewhat terrified at the results of this evening's experiments. Astonished at the wonderful power you have developed – and terrified at the thought that so much hideous and bad music may be put on record for ever . . .

and lived to hear it come true.

Gouraud failed, we may presume, to record the voice of the most talked-about personality of 1888, Jack the Ripper. But he did record the voice of the British Prime Minister, William Ewart Gladstone, and it proved to be Gouraud's most popular cylinder. Indeed it was so popular that street corner exhibitors of the phonograph, who were in the habit of faking cylinders, found it profitable to 'take off' the Grand Old Man.

As the initial wonder of the new talking machine wore off and while it was failing as a dictaphone, the public came to regard sound recording as no more than a scientific novelty. It was street corner exhibitors of the machine and nickelodeons, the forerunner of the modern juke-box, that perhaps did more than anything else to establish the word phonograph – and maintain it – in the public mind. However, only one element was lacking in order to make sound recording a part of everyday life: there was no cheap phonograph. In 1893, Edison's cheapest model retailed at $140 or £28. Three years later came the first of the Edison Home phonographs. This machine was advertised as 'the machine for the millions', but at $40 or £8 there were also millions who could not afford it. Columbia proved rather more effective in what was now a price war by introducing, at the same time, the Eagle phonograph, which sold at $10 or £2. Then in 1899 came the cheapest Edison machine of all, the pocket-sized Gem, which retailed at $7.50 or thirty shillings (£1.50).

Between 1896 and 1912, Edison turned out no less than 12,000 different titles on two-minute wax cylinders. These played at 160 revolutions per minute, had one hundred grooves to the inch and were roughly the same size as the inside of a toilet roll. In 1908 the number of grooves was increased to two hundred per inch, which provided four minutes of playing time. These were the only two successful kinds of cylinders: a prestigious grand concert cylinder with a diameter of 12.5 cm (5 inches) proved too fragile to be popular.

Edison poster, 1910. Note the prices. In an advertisement placed in The Times, 10 November 1910, the wage of £20–22 per year for a children's maid was by no means typical. That was the equivalent of twenty 78 sides – or two L.P.s – by Francesco Tamagno or Dame Nellie Melba. Sound recording did not become a truly mass medium until after the Second World War.

HOUSEHOLD SERVANTS WANTED.

(TWO LINES, 1s. ; EVERY EXTRA LINE, 6d.)

CHILDREN'S MAID REQUIRED, November 24th ; for country ; four children, ages 10 to 5 ; wages £20-£22 ; washing found, no beer ; age 24-26 ; good under-nurse might suit ; must be good needlewoman ; two in family and resident governess, seven indoor servants ; three miles from station and four from market town.—Apply, first by letter, to Mrs. Bendixson, Roxley Court, near Hitchin, Herts.

Cardboard box containers for a variety of early wax cylinders.

In the same period, despite the fact that the industry was beset by litigation and counter litigation, innumerable small companies mushroomed. The final decade of the last century and the first decade of this were the heyday of the cylinder phonograph and also, as events were to prove, its Indian summer. For even as the phonograph was establishing itself after an erratic start, it was joined and then ousted by the gramophone. There was nothing new about the idea of recording on disc. Charles Cros had considered the possibility of recording on both cylinder and disc. Edison had actually designed an experimental disc machine. But it was to Emile Berliner (1851–1929), a German immigrant to Washington, that the development of the gramophone owed its initial impetus. Dissatisfied with the results he had obtained from photo-engraving from a cylindrical surface, Berliner turned to recording on disc. He took out his first gramophone patent in November 1887, exactly ten years after Edison had produced his first phonograph.

Berliner's first phonograph had been based on Scott's phonautograph, whose stylus vibrated from side to side as opposed to up and down like a sewing machine needle. This was a matter of necessity not of choice, since the phonautograph merely traced a recording over a surface. But Berliner retained this principle of lateral recording. Instead of using the floor of the recording groove to register the sound waves, as the phonograph companies were doing, he used the walls of the groove, and this method reduced wear and the level of background noise. The gramophone had other advantages. Duplication of discs, once a master matrix or stamper had been made, was a comparatively simple process, and an indefinite number of copies could be made from a single matrix. The gramophone was also cheaper and simpler than the phonograph, as it dispensed entirely with the need for a feed screw during playback. Edison's objection to the disc machine was that the speed at which the groove revolves is never constant, but decreases as it approaches the centre. It still does.

The one advantage of the phonograph over the gramophone lay in the fact that it could be used for recording at home. It is interesting that this advantage did not save the phonograph from extinction. In 1878 the *Illustrated London News* put at the top of its list of virtues of the phonograph its potential for dispensing with letters: 'By its means . . . friends and lovers, sundered by half the globe, may communicate with each other by word of mouth.' But as time has shown, people do not normally wish to communicate by this means. Even with the introduction of easily-handled, unbreakable cassettes, tape-letters have not become common. The reason seems clear. Speech depends upon the relationship between speaker and listener for much of its character. Only

ile Berliner

The 'Trade-Mark' Model gramophone, 1898. This was Style No. 5, which retailed at £5.10.0 (£5.50).

BELOW *The English tenor Edward L (1845–1927) making a record for Gramophone Company. This photog appeared for the first time in* The Gra[p] *on 20 April 1907. How little was kn about the gramophone at this time ca judged by the quaint description periodical provided for its readers. ' piano and accompanist are raised o hollow sounding-box just behind the sin who stands a little distance from trumpet projecting from the wall, on other side of which is the record apparatus and plates of soft material which the precious sounds are for e imprisoned. These can only be relea when the possessor of a Gramophone pla a reproduction of the record in the form c black disc on the turn-table, and the nee again awakens the voice of the singer as rapidly turning disc engages the po traversing the wonderful sound wave line*

the professional broadcaster who has made a specialization of his art is likely to feel secure with his listener or audience at a remove.

Berliner, unlike the promoters of the phonograph, did not envisage his gramophone being used by industry and business houses. He aimed at entertainment. But at the beginning, while it remained hand-cranked, the gramophone sold only as a child's plaything. Not until Eldridge R. Johnson (1866–1945) had given the gramophone clockwork innards, and shellac had been substituted for rubber as the medium of recording, was the gramophone ready for wider commercial application. This was in 1897.

The next milestone lay not with recording techniques or design, but with recording artists. Looking through the Edison catalogue, one could be forgiven for being sceptical of those who maintain that modern pop represents a catastrophic decline in musical taste. Items such as 'I Think I Hear a Woodpecker Knocking at My Family Tree' or 'Afloat on a Five Dollar Note' could hardly be said to represent the apogee of mature musical taste.

The state of the recording industry before the turn of the century differed from the present in one crucial respect. It excluded the most important aural art form of the day. Today we have unlimited choice, though coupled with the rather confusing and hypocritical notion that a composition or a performer to be truly artistic must not also be popular. No such confusion existed in the Victorian mind. Opera was the great and universally popular art form. So long as the recording industry had the reputation of being the repository of trivia, opera singers were not

ɔVE *Toy Gramophone advertisement,*
ɔ. *This was not the use Berliner*
isaged for his invention. But with the
nograph companies well established, disc
ording was only likely to make progress
could offer its wares at a low price. It
s Eldridge Johnson who succeeded in
king the gramophone competitive by
igning a cheap clockwork motor.

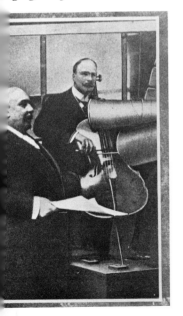

inclined to commit their voices to posterity, and until the talking machine received the imprimatur of the opera singer, it could not outgrow its reputation of being hardly more than a scientific toy.

More than with any other single individual, credit for breaking this vicious circle rests with the assiduous impresario Fred Gaisberg (1873–1951). But for Gaisberg, many of the greatest singers would never have recorded. And many more would have recorded only much later in their careers. Gaisberg's greatest catch was the voice of Enrico Caruso (1873–1921), whom he described as 'the answer to a recording engineer's dream'. Caruso was the answer to many dreams. To have his inimitable voice and top notes coming out of a brass trumpet became a pressing reason for investing in a gramophone. According to Joseph Murrells (*The Book of Golden Discs*):

> By 1952 the total royalties earned by his discs, both during his lifetime and since his death was over 3,500,000 dollars, representing the largest single royalty figure accrued by any artist in RCA-Victor's history up to that time.

These figures rather vindicated Gaisberg's recommendation in 1902 of investing £100 in the tenor as a fee for ten recordings, a proposition to which London headquarters had responded with the now famous telegram: 'Fee exorbitant – forbid you to record.'

Other singers followed Caruso's example of recording, although prejudice was still strong. Melba made a few experimental discs. 'Never again', she declared, and refused their publication. But that was not the end of her recording career. As she said, '. . . the gramophone people persisted. Never have I known such courtesy combined with such persuasion. They simply would not leave me alone.'

She was glad they persisted. The rewards were great. Francesco Tamagno, whom Verdi had chosen to create the role of Otello in 1887, insisted that his records should sell at a pound a piece. Melba, when she eventually allowed her records to be released, went one better and demanded that they should retail at one guinea. The results she found gratifying, not so much because she received proposals of marriage, prompted simply by hearing her voice on disc, but because her discs sold in thousands.

In 1905, the legendary soprano Adelina Patti (1843–1919) recorded for the first time. She was sixty-three and well past her prime, but no name carried greater prestige. The publication of her discs was heralded by advertisements taken, it is said, in two hundred papers, while record shops sported a notice which proclaimed: 'Patti sings here today.' And such was the response that Patti made a second series of recordings the following year. Sadly, few of her contemporaries followed her example. No recordings exist of the Viennese soprano Pauline Lucca (1841–1908), the American Clara Louise Kellogg (1842–1916) or

The legendary Adelina Patti adverti *Pears Soap. The social impact that* *opera had in Victorian times cannot* *illustrated better than by the fact that op* *singers were used in commercial advertis*

"*I have found PEARS' SOAP matchless for the hands and complexion.*"

The Polish tenor Jean de Reszke.

Lionel Mapleson, the librarian of the Metropolitan Opera. With the aid of an Edison phonograph mounted on the rafters above the Metropolitan stage, Mapleson managed to record live fragments of opera performances taking place far below. He carried out his experiments between 1901 and 1903, during the last years of Jean de Reszke's career. There are fifteen snatches of the tenor's voice extant.

Patti's great rival, the Hungarian Etelka Gerster (1855–1920). And the most important tenor of the second half of the Victorian Age, Jean de Reszke (1850–1925) refused to allow his records to be published. Other singers, often because their voices were in decline by the time they recorded, chose material which was unrepresentative of their art, or recorded too little for us to regard it as representative. Some singers, notably Marcella Sembrich (1855–1935) never felt at ease in front of the recording horn, and thus probably never achieved the same immediacy of communication that would have been the case in front of a live audience. And some voices, such as those of Lilian Nordica (1857–1914), Melba (1861–1931) and Emma Eames (1865–1952), did not take well to the acoustic process of recording.

Nevertheless, by the end of the Edwardian era, scores of operatic excerpts had been recorded by singers who had attained their prime before or at the turn of the century. So it is probably fair to say that the early gramophone has provided us with a representative sampling of the art of singing as it was understood and practised during the closing decades of the Victorian Age.

As more and more opera singers recorded on disc, a dichotomy between the gramophone and the phonograph began to emerge in the public mind. Initially, the phonograph had had the advantage of being the design promoted by the inventor of sound recording. But this advantage faded as the gramophone continued to gain prestige by its association with opera. In 1903, Columbia, playing safe, began to manufacture discs while retaining the emphasis on cylinder recordings. But this emphasis was quickly reversed, for the public demand was unmistakably for disc recordings, and in 1912 the company gave up the production of cylinders altogether.

Edison, however, persisted. To compete against the four minutes of playing time offered by the twelve inch disc, he marketed in 1908 his wax Amberol cylinder which also played for four minutes. In 1912 through the development of a hard wearing plastic, the Amberol was reconstituted and renamed the Blue Amberol. The quality of the reproduction from this cylinder was remarkably high; and as it was provided with an inner layer of plaster of Paris it was almost unbreakable. At the same time Edison sought out some of the most prestigious names in opera, Alessandro Bonci, Frieda Hempel, Lucrezia Bori and Selma Kurz among them. But these developments came too late and it was for a declining if faithful coterie that Edison continued to manufacture cylinders until 1929.

It has been well said that necessity is the mother of invention. It is also the mother of the application of invention. Although the microphone was invented the year before the phonograph, it was not used by the recording industry until 1925, almost half a century later. The date was not a chance one. Quite suddenly the recording companies had found themselves with a market in recession, and electrical recording was introduced to boost sales. Edison had envisaged electrical recording from the outset and the *Illustrated London News* of 3 August 1878 in its first article on the phonograph pointed out that:

> It should be borne in mind . . . this is but the baby-talk of an invention still in its infancy. When more matured, its voice will, of course, become stronger, and it may, perchance, be aided by the microphone, so that whispers breathed into its ear shall be thundered back.

How well, if unwittingly, had the periodical anticipated the marriage of the microphone and pop music. But if you had been a reader of *The Phonogram* during the 1890s you might have been excused for believing that any drawbacks associated with the acoustic process of recording were already a thing of the past. For example, in Vol. 1, No. 1, published in England in May 1893 *The Phonogram* declared that:

> In regard to any improvements likely to be made in the Phonograph, the instrument now for sale contains all the latest

improvements, and no changes are contemplated. The type will always remain the same, but such slight improvements as are deemed desirable will be added in the form of attachments . . .

By comparison, a reader of the *Gramophone* during the introduction of electrical recording might well have concluded that the new process offered no improvement at all on the old, indeed that it was retrogressive. The editor of the magazine, the novelist and gramophone enthusiast Sir Compton Mackenzie, listened to the first electrical recordings and reported to his readers in November 1925:

> The exaggeration of sibilants by the new method is abominable, and there is often a harshness which recalls some of the worst excesses of the past. The recording of massed strings is atrocious from an impressionistic standpoint. I don't want to hear symphonies with an American accent. I don't want blue-nosed violins and Yankee clarinets. I don't want the piano to sound like a free lunch counter.

His views were immediately echoed in 'Letters to the Editor' – very few disagreed with him. One correspondent wrote to say he found the Columbia issue of Parsifal excerpts 'ear-splitting, a continual humming roar pervading everything . . . The general tone of the orchestra is destroyed entirely by the new method of recording.' While another, less restrained, correspondent exclaimed, 'O, ye screeching Chinese mothers-in-law! I thought my old records would be worth only the "pudding" price of 6d each; now it's the reverse.'

In his review of the year, Mackenzie thought that:

> Rev. L. D. Griffith's discovery or re-discovery of the Lifebelt has opened up a new realm of reproduction for our readers. It is too early to say that the Lifebelt is the most important development of the gramophone in 1925, but first reports from our readers who are experimenting with it are as excited as those of the Editor in the London office . . .

A Lifebelt was a little piece of india-rubber tubing 'cut off a garden hose and enclosed in two curtain rings' and used as a connector between sound-box and horn. Not a word about electrical recording.

Predictably, a reaction soon set in. By April 1926 Mackenzie was writing: 'I don't know what my readers feel, but I feel that we are living on the verge of the most exciting times that the gramophone has yet experienced. The rapidity with which the new method of recording is being developed offers an enchanting prospect of the future . . .' And an historic event recorded live on 8 June 1926 convinced the editor beyond all reasonable doubt of the value of electrical recording:

> Of the new records, the most sensational are the two made at Covent Garden. Dame Nellie Melba, singing Mimi's Addío and her speech of farewell on the other side, definitely mark a new epoch in the power of the gramophone. . . . A record like this may not draw the sting of death, but it does rob the grave of a complete victory.

The acoustic process of recording did not pass, however, without some regrets. With certain singers – perhaps a majority – the old process was inclined to provide more 'body' to the voice simply by cutting out some of the higher harmonics. In the case of the coloratura soprano, Amelita Galli-Curci, this was certainly the opinion of a famous New York singing teacher J. H. Duval:

> Galli-Curci, of all the smaller voices, had the best emission and style. She has left us some admirable phonograph records. These records are better than her voice was in large auditoriums, where the lack of tone was very apparent.

Compton Mackenzie too, having heard her in concert, came away convinced that the gramophone and not her live performances was the source of her celebrity.

With electrical recording the gramophone had come of age. Virtually no instrument nor any combination of instruments was beyond its scope. Previously solo instruments and, more especially, the human voice recorded more faithfully than whole orchestras or even ensembles. In the early days of recording, instruments were difficult to record with any degree of realism. A Stroh violin – a resonator with a horn and four strings – was commonly substituted for a real violin; a bassoon was found to approximate to the tone of a 'cello, and a tuba to that of a double bass. The improvement made through the years in recording the voice was much less spectacular. Sir Thomas Beecham's saying that vocal recordings had not improved between 1910 and 1940 was hardly an exaggeration.

The real achievement of electrical recording lay in its ability to record instruments with the same fidelity as the human voice. A new public awareness of instrumental works developed. Interest in singing and vocal music had already begun to decline before the advent of electrical recording. Nevertheless, the gramophone almost certainly became a contributory factor in that decline. The medium had become a force for change. It did not become a force for maintaining the *status quo* –

although this has often been a role expected of the gramophone. Desmond Shawe-Taylor, for example, in an article on the gramophone, Fifth Edition of Grove, 1954, can express surprise at how

> . . . curious is our neglect of the great vocal records of the past, although the decline in singing, already perceptible in the early days of the gramophone, is by now so clear as to be capable of demonstration in terms of measurable fact. . . . Surely, as Reynaldo Hahn argued persuasively in one of the essays in his *Thèmes Varies*, aspiring singers ought to study with the utmost assiduity these surviving specimens of the grand manner. It is a typical paradox of our age that we should possess an aid to style which no previous generation has possessed, and should make so little use of it.

But if we learn anything from history, including vocal history, it is, indeed, that we do not learn anything from history. And to expect otherwise, it seems to me, is to misunderstand the function of the performer. Today, we tend to conclude that because the written score is permanent and fixed, so too should be the performance of it. But the performer relates, or should relate, not only to the score but to his audience. And the needs of a contemporary audience necessarily differ from those of the generation that preceded it. The Victorians understood this fact better than we, and so the Victorian singer was constrained by neither conductor nor orchestra in his exploitation of that relationship. Indeed, the conductor and orchestra were expected to serve, and to be subservient to, the singer's needs. Illustrative of this was the mounting of the opera *Guy Mannering* in the old Theatre Royal, Dublin on 12 May 1877. Taking a minor role was the Irish painter and singer Alexander Williams (1846–1930). He recalled in his unpublished memoirs:

> Sims Reeves was the tenor, and there was the usual apprehension amongst the performers as to whether the great man would really sing or not. At the last rehearsal in the middle of the day, he sent down his wife, who got a chair placed for her a couple of yards in front of R. M. Levy, the conductor. And whilst the band and chorus went through the work, she whistled Reeves' part, stopping the band and saying Mr Reeves would do so and so here, and giving the most minute details.

Unfortunately, the history of music has been equated with the history of composition to the almost total exclusion of those who performed it. This was, of course, inevitable, since before the turn of the century the

ns Reeves (1818–1900). He made his ratic debut in Guy Mannering *in 8, at Newcastle-on-Tyne. One may sume he therefore knew exactly what required of the orchestra when he came to g the same role in Dublin in 1877. His istling wife, the soprano Emma Lu-nbe, must have been well familiar with eeves' vocal ways by 1877, for they had n been married twenty-seven years. The d of autonomy that Reeves enjoyed uld be inconceivable today, and something s been lost as a result. Common sense ggests that there is a direct relationship tween the degree of credibility a performer 'll possess and the degree to which he is in arge of his own resources.*

only hard evidence for what took place beyond the reach of living memory lay in written scores, and scores alone yield only half a history. They tell us what was performed, but they cannot tell us how it was performed. The style inherent in any performance must always exceed what can be notated. This is especially true of singing, since no man-made instrument offers the same potential for variation as the human voice.

It is the performer who is the link between the composer's score and the public; he is the most direct touchstone of public taste. The style of his performance is likely to conform to the idiom of the score, but what is regarded as idiomatic is likely to be influenced by fashion. In a word, the performer is, above all else, a manifestation of contemporary taste.

The gramophone confirms this dramatically in the case of the vocal performer. For this century has seen not only a musical schism, but a vocal one as well. This schism effectively concluded a process which had already begun. The opera singer, who had already become less of a reflection of contemporary society after the First World War, ceased to be so altogether with the arrival of the microphone singer. No longer in possession of either a contemporary sound or a contemporary music, the opera singer lost his *raison d'être*. The predicament was a new one; and the result was a radical curtailment of the singer's prerogatives. As he was no longer a reliable touchstone of public taste, the performance derived less from the relationship between the singer and his audience. The elements of communication were now deemed to be exclusive to the score, and the singer, consequently, had little more to do than faithfully present the score. This amounted to a dramatic contraction of his previous function. Born of circumstance, the singer as *presenter* had replaced the singer as *performer*.

There was a time when the opera singer was furnished with no more than a skeletal composition, and gramophone history, had it only begun early enough, would have encompassed a third and prior age: the singer as composer. It was, however, in the age of the performer that the gramophone began, and within its scope the singer as performer is primarily a Victorian tradition, which extended for an indeterminate period into this century. It is with this tradition that the story of John McCormack, already seventeen by the time Queen Victoria died and barely out of his twenties at the outbreak of the First World War, begins.

NEW AND NOVEL

AN **ENTERTAINMENT** which presents the
newest and most wonderful Musical Instrument
and Talking Machine known to the present century

THE GRAPHOPHONE GRAND

This wonderful instrument must not for a moment be compared to the ordinary Talking Machines which have
been heard through the country for years.

The Graphophone Grand	PERFECTLY REPRODUCES THE HUMAN VOICE	DUPLICATES INSTRUMENTAL MUSIC
ACTUALLY ACCOMPLISHES WHAT HAS HITHERTO BEEN DEEMED **THE IMPOSSIBLE.**	**JUST AS LOUD,** **JUST AS CLEAR,** **JUST AS SWEET.**	WITH PERFECT **FIDELITY, TONE** and **BRILLIANCY.**

FILLS THE LARGEST AUDITORIUM OR CONCERT HALL AND NEVER FAILS TO CHARM ALL WHO HEAR IT

It is the talking machine long looked for, bringing the singer, the musician or the orchestra into the audible presence of the listener.
Those familiar with other types, but who have never listened to the **GRAPHOPHONE GRAND**, have no conception of its wonders.
The numbers rendered, while strictly first class, will range from grave to gay and will consist of the **LATEST MUSICAL SELECTIONS**
as played by **GILMORE'S** and **SOUSA'S BANDS** and the **MOST FAMOUS ORCHESTRAS**; **VOCAL SELECTIONS** by the **MOST NOTED**
SINGERS—operatic, sentimental and comic. **SPEECHES** which in their startling reproduction will astound all present and can be heard as
far or even farther than the original.

A CHOIR INVISIBLE. AN UNRIVALED MUSICAL FEAST.

Special arrangements have been made for magnifying the sound so that all may hear the entire concert while comfortably seated in
any part of the hall. Don't fail to take advantage of this opportunity and be sure to bring the children, for it will please them more than
anything that could be done for them.

PRICES OF ADMISSION: Adults_____ Children_____

EXHIBITION WILL BE GIVEN AT

_____

Doors Open at_____

*Advertisement for the Grapho-
ne. 'Perfectly reproduces the
man voice.' We may smile at
ir claims, but we have not
irely disposed of their standards.
ie telephone reports that are
rd daily on radio and television
ws bulletins have a quality of
roduction no higher than an early
x cylinder.*

1 THE BEGINNING

John McCormack was born in Athlone, Ireland, on 14 June 1884. In that year Adelina Patti was only forty-one and still in her prime; Jean de Reszke, at thirty-four, had just begun his career as a tenor in earnest; the Neapolitan tenor Fernando de Lucia, then twenty-three, made his debut in a concert performance of Boito's *Mefistofele*; the great Polish contralto, Ernestine Schumann-Heink, had been on the opera stage six years: Melba, then plain Helen Porter Mitchell, was within four years of her Covent Garden debut; Luisa Tetrazzini was a vocally precocious and doubtless bouncing thirteen-year-old, and Enrico Caruso was a treble chorister of eleven: Victorian singers or debutants all, whose paths McCormack in one way or another, was to cross.

His origins, however, in Athlone, a small town in the Irish midlands, were hardly promising. The town had no conspicuous musical tradition, and as a starting point for a singer it was remote in every sense from the international circuits of European and American opera houses. Even Dublin, the Irish capital, though only seventy-five miles from Athlone, would have been comparatively remote for the son of a mill foreman in those days. But if his background was humble, its disadvantages were not so great as is sometimes made out. At a time of much agrarian strife, few job opportunities and a long and widespread tradition of emigration, Athlone's population of seven thousand was actually on the increase through the employment offered by the local woollen mills. The tenor's parents, Andrew and Hannah McCormack, had moved from Galashiels in Scotland to Athlone. Attracted by the security the mills offered, they had moved into an area where improvement, if not rapid, was nevertheless in advance of many other areas of the country.

The river Shannon divides the town of Athlone into two counties. It

...e peaceful scene of the bridge at Athlone ...nning the River Shannon, circa 1900. ...the extreme left of the picture can be ...n the angular roofs of the woollen mills.

35

Hannah McCormack (née Watson), the tenor's mother. Of Scottish Presbyterian stock, she became a Roman Catholic on her marriage. In contrast to her husband and her famous son, Hannah was extremely reserved.

Andrew McCormack, the tenor's father. When John was bo was working as a labourer in the Athlone woollen mills. The did not recall him in an encouraging light: 'My father told should never amount to anything in this world.'

was on the east bank in the county of Westmeath that John Francis McCormack was born. He was one of five children to survive out of a family of eleven. Athlone had in 1871 a rate of illiteracy of almost 35 per cent. By 1891 the figure had been cut by more than half. Education was advancing and McCormack made the most of it. From the Marist Brothers in Athlone he won a scholarship to Summerhill College, Sligo, in 1896, when he was twelve. He maintained himself there with two further scholarships, showing a general aptitude for school subjects and excelling in mathematics and languages. In the school choir he gained a reputation for having a large voice, which suggests early vocal development and continual practice. The tenor himself said he could not remember a day at home when there was no singing. But neither home nor school provided him with a technical knowledge of music.

Nevertheless, by the time McCormack left Summerhill College in 1902, at the age of eighteen, a desire to make some sort of a career in singing had replaced an earlier notion of entering the priesthood. Parental pressure, however, made him sit for the Dublin College of Science scholarship examination. He was placed twenty-first, but only twenty scholarships were available, and after an abortive ten days or thereabouts as a clerk in the civil service, the tenor snapped up an offer of

McCormack amongst pupils of the M Brothers' School, Athlone. He is t from the left, second row from the b indicated with black circle. This is earliest known photograph of the tenor. was then about six years of age, which d the picture at about 1890.

The Palestrina Choir at St Patrick's Cathedral, Armagh, 1904. McCormack is fourth from the left in the back row. Three places further on, in a suit, is Edward Martyn who financed the choir. He is better remembered for his place in George Moore's autobiographical trilogy Hail and Farewell. *In the front row, fourth from the left, is Vincent O'Brien.*

a place in the Palestrina Choir of the Pro-Cathedral in Dublin. Under its choir-master, Vincent O'Brien, he took his first lessons in tonic sol-fa. The following year it was a reluctant debutant that O'Brien coached and coaxed for the *Feis Ceoil* or National Music Festival. At nineteen McCormack was the youngest competitor in the tenor section, but he took the gold medal by a comfortable margin. Another gold medallist was the soprano Lily Foley, shortly to become McCormack's wife.

It is sometimes thought that James Joyce, also an aspiring tenor, competed in the same Feis. It was in fact the following year that Joyce, encouraged by McCormack, made his bid for a gold medal. And he would have won it, had he made any kind of attempt at the compulsory sight-reading exercise. But his refusal even to attempt it automatically disqualified Joyce from the gold and he ended up with the bronze medal instead. His aspirations towards a professional singing career waned at this point, although he was offered free coaching by a well-known singing teacher, Benedetto Palmieri, an offer which was not extended to McCormack. McCormack and Joyce once appeared in the same concert at the Antient Concert Rooms, Great Brunswick Street (now Pearse Street) on 27 August 1904. They were not to meet again until the 1920s, but during the intervening period Joyce maintained a keen

McCormack, a diffident portrait – probably taken shortly after he left school. Josie Hoyle, the wife of a professional musician, recalled the nineteen year old tenor singing for the 'Dalkey Coal Fund' in 1903. He stood, in her own words, 'like a ploughboy', his arms, gauchly, hanging by his sides. McCormack was exceptionally ill at ease in public during his first years. But the voice was remarkably pure in tone and appears never to have had 'manufactured' quality about it.

interest in McCormack's career, avidly reading all available newsp critiques and personal stories. And when Joyce came to write *Finn Wake*, McCormack was a model for the character of Shaun the Pos Shaun's voice, Joyce wrote:

> . . . and cert no purer puer palestrine e'er chanted panangelical m the clouds of Tu es Petrus, not Michaeleen Kelly, not Ma O'Mario. . . .

'Puer palestrine' is, of course, a reference to the period the yo McCormack spent with the Palestrina Choir, and 'panangelical' r to the anthem 'Panis Angelicus', with words by St Thomas Aqu and music by César Franck. It was closely identified McCormack's career. The Palestrina boy's singing was not surpasse even 'Michaeleen Kelly', who as Michael Kelly sang in the production of Mozart's *Marriage of Figaro*, or 'Mara O'Mario', expands into two singers, Joseph O'Mara and the Italian tenor, M Giovanni Matteo, Cavaliere di Candia, better known simply as Ma probably the most celebrated tenor of the mid-nineteenth century. H praise indeed, although of the three tenors Joyce chose for comparis he could only have heard one. That was Joseph O'Mara (1866–19 whose career spanned the turn of the century. Like McCormack, he trained in Milan, and the two tenors appeared together in concert on

Announcement in the Freeman's Journal of the concert in the Antient Concert Rooms, in which James Joyce and McCormack both sang. It took place on 27 August 1904.

ANTIENT CONCERT ROOM
EXHIBITION OF IRISH
INDUSTRIES
AND
GRAND IRISH CONCERT,
TO-MORROW (Saturday) EVENING,
At 8 o'clock.

Artistes :—
Miss AGNES TREACY,
Miss OLIVE BARRY,
Madame HALL.
Miss WALKER (Marie Nic Shiubhlaigh).
Mr. J. C. DOYLE,
Mr. JAMES A. JOYCE, and
Mr. J. F. M'CORMACK.

Orchestra conducted by
Miss EILEEN REIDY, A.L.C.M., R.I.A.M.
Prices—3s. 2s. and 1s.
80193

Lily Foley – a carte photograph at the St Louis World Fair, 1904. *[befor]e leaving the fair, John and Lily [wer]e engaged. They kept it a secret on [accou]nt of their ages – they were then [twent]y and eighteen, respectively. Secrecy, [howe]ver, did not prevent her wearing her [engag]ement ring for this photograph.*

Miss Lily Foley
IRELAND'S EXPONENT OF GAELIC SONG
IRISH INDUSTRIAL EXHIBITION
Worlds Fair St. Louis, 1904
Murillo Studio, 1314 Olive St., St. Louis

least one occasion at the Theatre Royal, Dublin, in November 1906. O'Mara was well known in England and Ireland, but that is about as far as a comparison with McCormack could go. He had a reputation as a fine actor, and possessed a vigorous operatic style of singing and a rather biting, clarion tenor, so far as one may judge from his voice on record. Michael Kelly died in 1826 and Mario in 1883, when Joyce was not yet two years old. However, someone who did hear both Mario and McCormack, and who was not likely to have said she found a resemblance between the two voices without meaning it, was a Mrs Godfrey Pearse, Mario's own daughter.

Following their success at the Feis, both McCormack and Lily Foley were among the singers invited to cross the Atlantic in 1904 to sing at the St Louis Exposition. This was primarily a trade fair, but the visitor to the Irish Village, as it was called, had his eye regaled by a mock-up Blarney Castle and his ear by an Irish musical entertainment. McCormack soon had reservations. As Lily wrote in her biography of the tenor, *I Hear You Calling Me*:

> Everything was going well with the Irish Village until the management decided to add a comic Irish turn with a 'stage Irishman' to liven up the programme. We all protested. . . . Before any decision was reached John, with his quick temper, handed in his resignation, which was accepted just as promptly. I think they found John a rather difficult young man to handle. . . . This impulsiveness of John's remained to the end.

The story is repeated at length in Pierre Key's biography in the tenor's own words. For a boy just out of his teens and his career hardly begun, his resignation would seem extraordinary were it not for Lily's comment that, having gone out to the fair he then realised 'he was only losing time at work of this sort and he longed to get on with his serious study.' And that, the tenor had been advised, meant training in Italy.

He returned to Dublin, intent on raising the necessary funds. Three recording companies in London provided him with the unexpected opportunity to raise £100, the Edison and Edison-Bell Phonograph Companies for whom he recorded a series of ballads on two-minute wax cylinders, and the firm which later became HMV, then known as the Gramophone and Typewriter company (G & T), who recorded a similar series on discs. Copyright was a vague affair in those days, and it seems that McCormack had no trouble either in recording for three companies at the same time, or in repeating for the G & T series eight of the ten ballads he had already put on cylinder.

This was in the autumn of 1904, when McCormack was only twenty years old. From then until shortly before his death the tenor recorded almost every year. There have been singers, especially since the L.P. era, who have left more adequate representations of their repertoire on record; but McCormack's discography is unique among the great singers in having begun so early in his career. And his recording debut is of particular interest in that it took place before the tenor had had any vocal training in Italy.

In retrospect, McCormack had no illusions about his first efforts in front of the recording horn. 'Ye Gods, I heard one the other day', he wrote to Compton Mackenzie in the twenties, having heard one of his

The Gramophone & Typewriter L label of 'Killarney', 1904.

affectionate cartoon of Fred Gaisberg
Lissenden'. The suitcase was an apt
ol of his incessant travels across
pe.

old Edison cylinders, 'Too pathetic for words. The recording and recorder, oh, much too young.' Fred Gaisberg, impresario for the G & T Company, felt much the same way. In his autobiography, *Music on Record*, he recalled:

> It was not as a celebrity but as a provincial singer of Irish Ballads that the twenty-one year old John McCormack was brought to my studio in the autumn of 1905. [The year was, in fact, 1904 and the tenor was twenty.] Untidy, unkempt, sporting a much worn overcoat with a moth-eaten collar, I noted especially his bad teeth, a thing his future teacher, Maestro Sabatini, straightway made him correct before he would enlist him as one of his pupils.
>
> Concerning the ten discs he recorded that day . . . [McCormack said he was contracted to make twenty-five and MacDermott Roe's discography lists eighteen] I never did feel happy. . . . The records never gave the slightest indication of the future golden voice that was destined to play so large a part in spreading world wide the vogue of the gramophone. . . . At least the fees helped to finance John's studies in Italy with Sabatini, who in a few short months wrought a miracle and turned an uncouth singer of songs into an opera artist.

The difference between the recordings McCormack made before going to Italy and those he made in 1906, having had less than a year's tuition with Sabatini, is considerable; yet it would be going too far to say that they bear no comparison. Almost all the great singers have sounded wholly individual and quite unlike any other singer. McCormack was no exception in this respect. He sounds unmistakable in his first recordings, and hardly less so than in any he made later. Predictably, what the 1904 recordings lack, and which is revealed for the first time in 1906, is any indication of vocal schooling. One is immediately aware of the frequency with which he uses a sob – three times, no less, on the word 'pining' in the G & T 'Molly Bawn' and on both 'pining' and 'calling' in the Edison version. This is very untypical of his later work.

Even more conspicuous in the 1904 recordings is his use of portamenti. Although his phrasing has an undeniable sense of shape, the portamenti he employs are all exaggerated. He does not use this device sparingly, as one would expect with an ornament, but unremittingly, which suggests a reason other than simply a desire to embellish the vocal line. It seems probable that in this period the tenor was not capable of sustaining a vocal line without resort to 'leaning' on congenial notes in each phrase. In the G & T 'Come Back to Erin', for instance, the highest and lowest notes are consistently stressed, while between the two the tenor hurries

along with a rather punctuated rhythm and frequent scooping. This style of singing in which the top and bottom notes of a line are stressed – sometimes called 'terraced' singing – is characteristic of the Irish folk-singer and on these first records McCormack's style might seem influenced by his early experiences. He would have heard many folk-singers in Athlone and may even have sung in a folk idiom himself during his childhood and early youth. The possibility of an indirect folk influence cannot be entirely discounted, but I think it unlikely that there was conscious imitation on McCormack's part. Although he shows an affinity for passing notes as the folk-singer does, he does not hold the

ABOVE AND LEFT *Pathé etched-label 'Come Back to Erin' and 'The Dear Li Shamrock'. Unlike most other discs, Pa discs operated on the 'hill 'n' dale' princip and many had to be played from the in groove to the outer.*

stressed notes for anything like the duration one would expect of a folk-singer. Nor does he employ quarter-tones as a folk-singer would be certain to do. As Herbert Hughes observed in a preface to one of his collections of Irish folk-songs: 'Over and over again I have found it impossible to write down a tune that has been sung or played to me, for the simple reason that our modern notation does not allow for intervals of less than a semitone.'

Having shared the concert platform with such notable Dublin recitalists as J. C. Doyle and Agnes Treacy, McCormack would have been thoroughly familiar with accomplished and smooth legato singing and a well tempered scale, and these singers would almost certainly have been among his early models. But vocal style cannot exceed vocal resource. The likelihood is that his habitual use of portamenti in 1904 was a compensation – or over-compensation – for a voice not yet sufficiently developed to sustain an even legato line. It made for a curious, hybridized style of singing.

There is nothing to suggest that in 1904 McCormack had as much as set himself the goal of clear enunciation. Very possibly he had yet to hear English eloquently sung (how rarely one does). And one forgets that in those pre mass-media days one was limited to models within one's own environment. It seems likely that McCormack did not recognize the verbal possibilities of song until he appeared in London concerts in 1907 and came into contact with such singers as Harry Plunket Greene. Interestingly, the rich brogue inseparable from the later McCormack was not apparent in 1904. The vowels are flat and lustreless; and so far as one may judge from the tenor's own spoken introductions on cylinder, he then possessed a relatively mild midland-Irish accent, possibly flattened by his removal to Dublin. English critics, who were by no means always enamoured of his brogue, tended to regard his vowels as Italian in origin. The critic of *The Times* (12 October 1912), for example, after a performance of Mendelssohn's *Elijah* at the Birmingham Festival, complained of his 'tendency to make English words ridiculous by singing the vowels as though they were Italian ones.' But clearly, this is to overestimate the importance McCormack's fluency in Italian could have exerted on his English pronunciation – no Italian tenor who has sung in English ever sounded like an Irishman! Compared with McCormack's original 1904 pronunciation, the later development of the brogue consisted of comparatively minor adjustments: a rounding of the vowels rather than a relocation of them. His use of the brogue was not only an assertion of his Irish identity but was also a valuable expedient for vocal placement; a feature of broad vowels likely to have been borne in upon him during his period of study in Italy.

What these early 1904 records do not easily explain, however, is the reputation that the twenty-year-old tenor had already acquired, and there is plenty of evidence to suggest that it was, even then, considerable. For example, after the concert in the Antient Concert Rooms of 27 August 1904, in which several well-known Dublin singers participated, *The Evening Telegraph* of 29 August reported:

> Mr J. F. McCormack was the hero of the evening. It was announced as his last public appearance in Ireland, and the evident feeling of the audience at the parting seemed to unnerve him a good deal. . . . The audience seemed as if it would never hear and see enough of him, and twice he had to respond to triple encores, while he was recalled times almost without number.

In his report to the Feis Ceoil committee, the adjudicator in the vocal section on this occasion, Luigi Denza, then a singing teacher at the Royal Academy of Music in London, only singled out McCormack. And his impression was unequivocal:

> The tenor, to whom was awarded first prize, has a fine voice, and gives promise of developing into a singer of exceptional merit and brilliancy with a few years of conscientious study.

But it is perhaps Stanislaus Joyce – James Joyce's brother – who brings us closest to the young McCormack. In his *Dublin Diary* of 1904 he wrote: 'I called McCormack's voice a "white voice" – it is a male contralto', a remark which suggests a voice of unusual purity.

The timbre of the voice eluded these early records, but what repeated playings do reveal is that the tenor, even as early as 1904, was producing his voice in a manner which was completely free of *extraneous muscular tension*. This suggests that his instinct was certain from the beginning; and indeed, only so certain an instinct could account for the limpid and perfect focus of tone that the gramophone clearly reveals only a few years later. The most conspicuous problem for the tenor in 1904 was that his instinct for singing without tightness or unwarranted muscular tension in the throat affected the organs of articulation, which were so relaxed as to be almost inoperative.

While in London for the purpose of making these records, McCormack attended a performance of *La Bohème* at the Royal Opera, Covent Garden, and heard Enrico Caruso for the first time, an experience that he never forgot. 'That voice rings in my ears after thirty-three years,' he wrote for his projected autobiography, 'the memory of its beauty will never die.' McCormack's love for Caruso's voice and, indeed, for the tenor himself was lifelong. Almost inevitably, he spent a period of his early career trying to emulate the Italian. This can be demonstrated clearly on record, and nowhere better than on McCormack's recording of 'Celeste Aida' made for the Odeon Company in 1909. The vehement manner in which he attacks and holds the high B flat beginning the phrase: '*ergerti un trono vicino al sol*' is as like Caruso as anything one is likely to find outside the Italian's own discography. Of course, had McCormack's attempts to emulate Caruso's top notes become habitual, his voice would have been spoilt very quickly. But in the short term it almost certainly worked to his advantage. McCormack's inclination was always to minimize the breath pressure on the vocal chords and this, in addition to the fact that his vocal range was not large, created a tendency for his voice to break in the top register during his first years in opera. His early recordings for the Odeon Company show a reluctance or an inability to 'cover' on the high notes above A. A more deft attack, the art of covering in the top register, and consequently a greater security at the top, were almost certainly taken from Caruso. Dismissing early the more virile and resonant kind of sound heard, for example, in the Odeons 'Celeste Aida', 'On with the Motley' and Leoncavallo's 'Mattinata', McCormack turned to producing a delicate top with the resonance finely tapered as the voice moved upwards. The duet 'Del Tempio al Limitar', from *The Pearl Fishers*, recorded in 1911 with the Sicilian baritone Mario Sammarco, demonstrates the essential McCormack top. As the American critic Henry Pleasants has aptly written: '[The two B flats,] especially the coldly attacked first of them, eight measures before the end, are as thrillingly perfect as any in the entire catalog of tenor recording.'

This kind of singing was still in the future when on 13 January 1906, after only three months' tuition with Sabatini, the tenor made his operatic debut in the title role of Mascagni's *L'Amico Fritz*, at the Teatro Chiabrero, Savona. He recalled 'being scared stiff at the high B flat and knowing that I could not possibly be heard over what seemed to me then a very large orchestra, I just opened my mouth wide, struck a dramatic attitude but made no sound. The audience, thinking they heard a beautiful B flat, insisted on an encore.' (*I Hear You Calling Me*)

He was less fortunate while singing the part of Faust at the Teatro Verdi, Santa Croce sull' Arno. His voice cracked on a high note and, not wishing to experience the reaction of the audience, he fled the stage. The same trouble beset the tenor when he auditioned before Giulio Gatti-Casazza at La Scala, and was consequently turned down. Unemployment followed a few engagements in minor opera houses.

Now a married man and with his wife expecting her first child,

McCormack in the title role of L'Amico Fritz, in which he made his operatic debut on 13 January 1906, in Savona.

Poster announcing Boosey Ballad Concert, Queen's Hall, 1 March 1907. McCormack virtually established his reputation as a ballad singer at this concert, when he introduced Samuel Liddle's 'A Farewell'. The newcomer did not quite please everyone. Francis Toye ruefully recalled, in his autobiography, what he had written in March 1907: 'There was a new tenor called McCormack with lots of voice but no brains.' The naiveté of the tenor's style prior to his Covent Garden debut may have accounted for that impression.

McCormack decided to leave Italy for London. It was to prove, very quickly, to have been the right decision. Late in 1906 or early in 1907, McCormack moved into lodgings at 12a, Torrington Square. Shortly afterwards, Perceval Graves, then a law student, took lodgings in the same house. He recalled:

McCormack had a top floor bed-sitter and the use of a lovely little Bord piano on which he taught himself to play. He had a tremendous power of concentration. When I first knew McCormack he didn't give a damn how he dressed. How could he, considering that without private means he had to work for every penny he earned.

We were lucky in our landlord, Jim Balmer . . . who was fond of good music and a popular member of the Choughs, an amateur music club, and in John's early days, when he was just able to rub along, Jim Balmer put quite a few engagements in his way.

But I think he first came into his own in London when our landlord lent him five pounds to buy a fur coat with and which he repaid just as soon as he could. It gave him a great sense of comfort and well being.

John and I used to walk down the Strand, the singer sporting a Trilby hat, somewhat the worse for wear. He generally carried a packet of boiled sweets in his pocket. Except for very rare occasions he was a non-smoker.

Poster for a National Sunday League Concert at the Queen's Hall, London, 1907. The recording McCormack made in 1911 of 'Ah, Moon of My Delight', from Lehmann's song cycle In a Persian Garden, reveals the exquisite purity and focus of tone that his voice possessed in this period. It is also one of his most perfectly judged recordings.

His first major London engagement came on 1 March 1907, when he sang at a Boosey Ballad Concert in Queen's Hall. The official accompanist, Samuel Liddle, had suggested to the tenor that he should introduce an entirely new ballad at the concert, and offered him his own composition 'A Farewell', with words by Charles Kingsley. McCormack's success with this song was immediate. It became a popular drawing-room piece and the singer was assured of further engagements from Arthur Boosey. Private engagements in soirée and salon began to come his way. Graves remembered the ageing Duchess of Devonshire who, with the aid of a hearing trumpet, was apparently a good judge of the singing voice, listening intently:

to Stephen Adams' impassioned ballad 'Roses', in which McCormack gave out a ringing A natural with tremendous conviction. This, with other numbers, no doubt from his Irish repertory, did the trick. The old lady was so delighted that she told all her friends and influential acquaintances all about the young minstrel, who soon became swamped with lucrative engagements.

McCormack also appeared at Queen's Hall in Henry Mills' National Sunday League Concerts, 'Sunday Evenings for the People', taking part in Liza Lehmann's song cycle *In a Persian Garden* as early as May 1907. Shortly after this performance, he took the boat to Dublin to sing in *Cavalleria Rusticana* and *Faust* with the Dublin Amateur

John McCormack and his patron, Sir John Murray Scott, c. 1908. In the presence of Sir John the tenor looks uncharacteristically meek.

Operatic Society under the direction of Barton McGuckin. He was advertised, as none of the other principals was, with his name in bold print. 'J. F. McCormack,' as he was still called, 'will make his first appearance in English opera, since returning from Italy as Turiddu in *Cavalleria Rusticana*, under the patronage of the Lord and Countess of Aberdeen', ran the advertisement in *The Irish Times*. Evidently McCormack was the prime attraction. Vocally he did not disappoint. The same paper reported that the 'Siciliana' was 'a strong effort, the high notes being given with power and sweetness, and the closing diminuendo marked with tender feeling. . . .' Less impressive was his acting: 'When the challenge was conveyed to Alfio by the ear-biting expedient, the audience might have construed the action as a loving embrace.'

If these performances in Dublin were not McCormack's first forays into amateur opera, they were certainly his last. Apart from his year in Italy, the tenor never really knew obscurity. He had left Dublin a well-known local singer, spent less than two years in Italy, where Sabatini seems to have acted as a catalyst in the development of an extraordinary

Cormack as Turiddu in Mascagni's Cavalleria Rusticana.

natural talent, and quickly made his mark as a ballad singer in London. It was while singing at Queen's Hall that he was heard and admired by Sir John Murray Scott, a man of means and influential in musical circles. He, according to Lily McCormack, probably influenced John McCormack's career more than anyone else. It was through Sir John that the young tenor was introduced to and obtained an audition with Harry Higgins, the general manager of Covent Garden. It is said that Higgins expressed doubts about the size of the voice and that Sir John countered his misgivings by suggesting that the orchestra play softer. (A

Royal Opera Covent Garden
Lessee and Manager ... Mr. FRANK RENDLE
Autumn Opera Season, 1907
Mr. FRANK RENDLE
in conjunction with
THE GRAND OPERA SYNDICATE, LTD.
General Manager, Mr. NEIL FORSYTH
Musical Director, Mr. PERCY PITT

THIS EVENING'S PERFORMANCE

Saturday, October 26th, at 8
MASCAGNI'S Opera
CAVALLERIA RUSTICANA
(IN ITALIAN)

Turiddu	...	...	Mr. JOHN McCORMACK
Alfio ...	...	...	Signor SCANDIANI
Lola ...	...	...	Signora ZOFFOLI
Lucia ...	...	...	Signora BORGHI
Santuzza	...	...	Mlle. PRYHN
	Conductor	...	Signor PANIZZA

Followed by LEONCAVALLO'S Opera
PAGLIACCI
(IN ITALIAN)

Nedda	...	...	Mlle. DE LIS
Canio	...	...	Signor BASSI
Tonio	...	...	Signor SAMMARCO
Beppe	...	...	Signor BADA
Silvio ...	...	..	Mr. ALBERT GARCIA
	Conductor	...	Signor PANIZZA

suggestion which would not come amiss today on occasion.) How critical the presence of McCormack's patron may have been on that occasion we shall never know; McCormack himself considered he was generally a poor performer at auditions. At any rate, on 15 October 1907, in the role of Turiddu, McCormack became, at twenty-three, the youngest tenor ever to sing a major role at Covent Garden. Perceval Graves was there:

> It was for me a wildly exciting night. Two hundred and fifty of us marched from the old Irish Club in Charing Cross Road to Covent Garden, marshalled by old Sam Goddes, the proprietor, to form a powerful Hibernian claque. The Italian claques were powerful enough up there during the Italian season, so why not an Irish contingent? I can't remember where we all sat but I distinctly

recollect the hush that fell over the audience when, with the curtain down and the house dark, we listened intently for the first notes of the deathless Siciliana, from the moment the strains began to filter through the curtain to the expectant audience to the end of the aria. And we realized that another star had arrived, no meteor either, but a planet that would beam brightly and steadfastly in the musical firmament. That top C of his, whether ringing out with a silver resonance or subdued to a delicate mezza voce, was unsurpassable.

Of his acting, it is kinder to say nothing except that he was just himself, a simple and sincere Irish singer, incapable of interpreting the Sicilian way of life.

The *Daily Telegraph* noted that 'he certainly made a favourable impression'; and the paper was somewhat bemused by the fact that, although the same operas had already been seen this season, this time:

... there was a house of far larger dimensions than before. And not only was the assembled multitude greater, their enthusiasm was on a par, and the scene at the close of the first-named was one not often witnessed in our chief opera house. We need not stop to argue as to how much or how little of this was due to love of the operas themselves. If it was in support of Mr John McCormack, a young Irish singer of great promise, who as Turiddu took his first operatic plunge, who shall hold up his hand against it?

The Times was more reserved, finding the visual side of his performance quite incapable of meeting the demands of the part:

Apart from the weakness of his first entrance, it needs an experienced actor to play the part of the spoilt boy consistently. Mr McCormack ... showed his inexperience by strolling about the stage and allowing himself ineffective actions. Moreover, in the first act the quality of his voice did not compare well with that of Mlle Bryhn.

However, in the second act *The Times* found the tenor 'more at ease and he used his voice with admirable effect.'

The previous year, 1906, McCormack had signed a contract with the Odeon Company to record a maximum of twelve sides per year over six years, at £150 per annum. With the first of these Odeons there is evidence of a sense of craft not present in 1904. But it is over the four years 1906 to 1910 that his craftsmanship and his powers as a communicator developed with a rapidity which has probably no parallel in the annals of the gramophone. The 'Siciliana', which he recorded close to his debut, either late in 1907 or early in 1908, is his first operatic title. It is perhaps the first record to have recognizable associations with the tenor's maturity, although it has not been accepted without criticism. In *The Record Collector* of April 1968, for instance, Paul Morby goes so far as to say:

> If he sang the whole opera even as well as he sings the Siciliana in English on the 1908 Odeon, the performance must have been an embarrassment to the public and to his Lola.

But surely this is a harsh judgement. True, as with many of the tenor's records, one has to make do with a spirited performance as opposed to a dramatic one; but if there is a lack of passion, there is, nevertheless, a feel for words which is not likely to be found in another English version. And there are other qualities: almost for the first time, we can observe the immaculate way in which McCormack learnt to make his attacks and line endings. The delineation of line is never in doubt, and is far more scrupulous than one would normally expect to hear from an Italian tenor. The long drawn out 'Ah', with which the aria ends, is both rhythmically buoyant and beautifully controlled. This is the emergent McCormack without a doubt.

Three weeks after his debut at Covent Garden, on 6 November 1907, McCormack appeared as Don Ottavio in Mozart's *Don Giovanni*. This time, *The Times* of 8 November had no reservations and described his performance as:

> A great success; the songs – both of them were given – were sung with fine taste and vocal finish, while the timbre of the voice is exactly what is wanted in the part.

The *Daily Telegraph* noted that: 'It is easy enough to say [he] has much to learn', but found he sang 'Dalla Sua Pace' 'with a sense of phrasing that was exquisite.' It was an astonishing achievement for a twenty-three year old tenor singing his second role in a major opera house. On his honeymoon in July 1906, with his young wife, McCormack had watched Caruso from the gallery at Covent Garden and vowed: 'If I ever get my foot down there it'll take a hell of a lot to get it off.' It was to take a world war.

LEFT *McCormack as Don Ottavia*, and BELOW *Covent Garden programme for* Don Giovanni, *6 November 1907*. McCormack's recording of 'Il Mio Tesoro' could hardly be more highly regarded, and deservedly so. But it has almost certainly led us to overestimate the tenor's impact as Don Ottavio. After the first performance of Don Giovanni at Covent Garden in four years, The Times gave the honours to Mlle. Destinn, 'the most excellent' in the cast, while remarking of McCormack that he 'was allowed both his arias, sang them well, and no more can be expected of a Don Ottavio.' The following year, when he again sang the role, The Times spoke of his 'easy singing . . . always pleasant if rather monotonous in quality.' The Daily Telegraph in 1909 went no further than to say that he 'answered effectively' as Don Ottavio. McCormack received very much more enthusiastic reviews in other roles while at Covent Garden. His Don Ottavio was more highly thought of in America, when he sang the role with the Boston Opera Company.

Royal Opera Covent Garden

Lessee and Manager ... Mr. FRANK RENDLE

Autumn Opera Season, 1907

Mr. FRANK RENDLE
in conjunction with
THE GRAND OPERA SYNDICATE, LTD.
General Manager, Mr. NEIL FORSYTH
Musical Director, Mr. PERCY PITT

THIS EVENING'S PERFORMANCE

Wednesday, November 6th, at 8

MOZART's Opera

DON GIOVANNI

(IN ITALIAN)

Donna Anna	...	Mme. LITVINNE
Donna Elvira	...	Mme. LEJEUNE
Zerlina	...	Mlle. LALLA MIRANDA
Leporello	...	Signor LUPPI
Don Ottavio	...	Mr. JOHN McCORMACK
Mazetto	...	Signor WIGLEY
Il Commendatore	...	Mr. FRANK ARTHUR
Don Giovanni	...	Signor SAMMARCO
Conductor	...	Mr. PERCY PITT

2 THE OPERA SINGER

Within the space of a single season, McCormack had become a *primo tenore* at Covent Garden. Engaged for the following, more prestigious, Royal Opera or Summer Season of 1908, he sang thereafter in every Royal Opera Season until the outbreak of the First World War, when the Opera House temporarily closed down. By that time, he had appeared at Covent Garden in fifteen different operas; and only in the role of Cassio, which he sang to the Otello of Giovanni Zenatello in 1908, and of Leo Slezak in 1909, did McCormack ever sing a role secondary to another tenor.

It was no mean achievement, not least because he was not from the European continent. As *The Graphic*, in its issue of 26 October 1907, wryly remarked:

> If our grandfathers were able to arise from their graves and once more take their places in their old stalls at the opera . . . [and] Covent Garden should ask them to listen to the singing of . . . a homely John McCormack [it] would seem to them a piece of unbounded impertinence . . . though they would, no doubt, be ready and willing enough to applaud the efforts of M. Max Cormacski, the eminent Polish tenor.

Walter Hyde, an English tenor, was not so lucky. As Harold Rosenthal, in *Two Centuries of Opera at Covent Garden*, pointed out:

> He was heard as Pinkerton and 'sang with such excellent tone and expression that the result was never in doubt'; however, being a beginner and English, he was given little other work during the season, despite the inadequacy of both Marak and another newcomer, Edoardo Garbin. . . .

McCormack as Cavaradossi in Tosca.

Covent Garden programmes of some of the operas in which John McCormack appeared, 1908–1914.

Royal Opera Covent Garden
Proprietors . The Grand Opera Syndicate, Ltd.
General Manager . Mr. NEIL FORSYTH
Musical Director . Mr. PERCY PITT

THIS EVENING'S PERFORMANCE

Monday, May 30th, at 8.30
PUCCINI'S OPERA
LA BOHÈME
In Italian

Mimi .	Mme. MELBA
Musetta .	Mlle. SYMIANE
Rodolfo .	Mr. JOHN McCORMACK
Marcello .	Signor SAMMARCO
Colline .	Signor MARCOUX
Schaunard .	Signor MALATESTA
Benoit }	Signor GIANOLI-GALLETTI
Alcindoro }	
Parpignol .	Signor ZUCCHI

The Bellew and Stock Choir

Conductor . Signor CAMPANINI

Stage Manager . M. ALMANZ

For future Announcements see inside.

Royal Opera Covent Garden
Proprietors . The Grand Opera Syndicate, Ltd.
General Manager . Mr. NEIL FORSYTH
Musical Director . Mr. PERCY PITT

[1910]

THIS MORNING'S PERFORMANCE

Thursday, July 28th, at 2
DÉLIBES' OPERA
LAKMÉ
(In Italian)

Lakmé .	Mme. TETRAZZINI
Mallika .	Mlle. BOURGEOIS
Ellen .	Mlle. SYMIANE
Rose .	Mlle. EGENER
Mrs. Benson .	Mme. BÉRAT
Gerald .	Mr. JOHN McCORMACK
Nilakantha .	Mr. EDMUND BURKE
Frederic .	M. CRABBÉ
Hadji .	Signor ZUCCHI

Première Danseuse Mlle. OPALFVENS
Conductor . Signor PANIZZA

Stage Manager . M. ALMANZ

For future Announcements see inside.

Royal Opera Covent Garden
Proprietors . The Grand Opera Syndicate, Ltd.
General Manager . Mr. NEIL FORSYTH
Musical Director . Mr. PERCY PITT

[1912]

THIS EVENING'S PERFORMANCE

Saturday, June 1st, at 8.15
ROSSINI'S OPERA
IL BARBIERE DI SIVIGLIA
(In Italian)

Rosina .	Mme. TETRAZZINI
Bertha .	Mme. A. L. BERAT
Basilio .	Signor VANNI MARCOUX
Bartolo .	Signor POMPILIO MALATESTA
Fiorello .	Signor SAMPIERI
Conte d'Almaviva .	Mr. JOHN McCORMACK
Figaro .	Signor G. MARIO SAMMARCO
Sergente .	Signor DANTE ZUCCHI

Conductor . Signor ETTORE PANIZZA

Stage Manager . M. ALMANZ

McCormack as Cavarodossi in Tosca.

Royal Opera Covent Garden
Proprietors . The Grand Opera Syndicate, Ltd.
General Manager . Mr. NEIL FORSYTH
Musical Director . Mr. PERCY PITT

[1914]

THIS EVENING'S PERFORMANCE

Friday, June 26th, at 8
BOITO'S OPERA
MEFISTOFELE
(In Italian)

Mefistofele .	ADAMO DIDUR
Marguerite .	CLAUDIA MUZIO
Elena .	ROSINA RAISA
Faust .	JOHN McCORMACK
Nereus }	DANTE ZUCCHI
Wagner }	
Martha .	LOUISE BERAT
Pantalis .	RUBY HEYL
Première Danseuse .	FELYNE VERBIST
Conductor .	GIORGIO POLACCO

Stage Manager . M. FERNAND ALMANZ

For future Announcements see inside.

Royal Opera Covent Garden
Proprietors . The Grand Opera Syndicate, Ltd.
General Manager . Mr. NEIL FORSYTH
Musical Director . Mr. PERCY PITT

[1914]

THIS EVENING'S PERFORMANCE

Thursday, July 9th, at 8.30
PUCCINI'S OPERA
TOSCA
(In Italian)

Floria Tosca .	EMMY DESTINN
Mario Cavaradossi .	JOHN McCORMACK
Il Barone Scarpia .	DINH GILLY
Cesare Angelotti .	GEORGE EVERETT
Il Sagrestano .	POMPILIO MALATESTA
Spoletta .	DANTE ZUCCHI
Sciarrone .	MICHELE SAMPIERI
Un Pastore .	GERTRUDE BLUMENTHAL
Un Carceriere .	GIUSEPPE PINI

The Bellew and Stock Choir
Conductor . GIORGIO POLACCO

Stage Manager . M. FERNAND ALMANZ

For future Announcements see inside.

One might have thought that the size of McCormack's voice would have been a decisive factor against his acceptance in a house as large as Covent Garden. It was not, apparently, the smallest voice to be heard there; when he appeared with Alice Nielsen in *Madame Butterfly* in 1913, *The Times* noted that he 'tempered his voice with discretion in the duets'. But in all likelihood, McCormack's voice did not compare in power with any of the Italian tenors who sang regularly in London. Yet the press, after his first season, was rarely critical of the size of his voice. The gramophone suggests why.

McCormack's sense of dynamic proportions was acute; and one feels that he retained full possession of his powers even in full voice. The security of his vocal placement and the lightness with which he applied breath to the vocal chords provided him with a vocal line that was never 'smudged'. A McCormack phrase can be followed effortlessly, and that has much to do with the level of volume that the listener will find satisfactory.

By 1913, after a performance of *La Bohème*, *The Times* of 23 May could write of his voice:

> Its development since he first appeared here is very striking, and the combined strength and beauty of its quality now places him in the front rank of tenors.

Naples, however, did not react with quite the same enthusiasm, when he paid a return visit to Italy in the spring of 1909. Through the influence of the baritone, Mario Sammarco – with whom he had struck up a friendship in London – McCormack made his debut at the San Carlo as Alfredo in *La Traviata* on 19 March 1909, and followed this up six days later with a performance of the Duke of Mantua in *Rigoletto*. His press was by no means unapproving. *Il Mattino* of 20 March, for example, wrote after his performance in *Traviata*: '*Il tenore Mac Kormack fece nel suo debutto ottima impressione. Cantò con buoni mezzi vocali e fu cordialmente festeggiato dal pubblico.* (He made an excellent impression at his debut, singing with good vocal means and was cordially applauded by the public.) While after *Rigoletto*, the same paper remarked: '. . . *Mac Kormack che ha insinuanti qualità vocali messe in evidenza in più parti dell'opera verdiana.*' (Having ingratiating vocal talents, he put into relief the greater part [of his role] in the Verdi opera.) But McCormack found his audience lukewarm, and the major success that he had set his heart upon did not materialize. It would, perhaps, have been surprising if it had. As little as Covent Garden, at that time, was disposed to favour native talent, the San Carlo rarely responded to anything else. And McCormack did not have the qualities that were likely to endear him to a Neapolitan audience. In London, he was found to be 'not a particularly dashing Duke, and does not throw off his two impudent songs as the Southern-born singer does. . . .' (*The Times*, 28 May 1912) while the *Illustrated London News* had already described his Duke, in 1908, as a 'rather respectable roué'. These were not shortcomings that were likely to be overlooked by an Italian audience.

Less than a generation later, in the twenties, an Irish soprano, Margaret Burke-Sheridan, did score a series of notable triumphs at Naples and Milan, particularly in the operas of Puccini. The unlikeliness of a foreigner succeeding thus was not lost on the *Daily Telegraph*. After she had made an appearance as Madame Butterfly at the San Carlo in 1927, the paper noted that the critics were as enthusiastic as the audience, 'which is saying a good deal in the land of the "bel canto", where jealousy of the foreigner is a ruling passion.' But Burke-Sheridan had just those qualities which ingratiate themselves with an Italian audience and which McCormack lacked: an immense amount of vocal stamina and power, a dramatic temperament, and a fair measure of sensuousness in her vocal make-up. McCormack's tone was eminently suave, but not at all sensual. His timbre might be described as having been of a unique kind of non-secular purity, far removed from the colour of Italian voices. And though spirited and spontaneous, McCormack rarely sounded dramatic *in an Italian sense*. The qualification is a necessary one, because there is plenty of material outside the Italian repertoire where he does impart a considerable sense of drama and even fervour; for example, in Bix's 'The Trumpeter', Balfe's 'Come into the Garden, Maud', and Rachmaninov's 'O, Cease thy singing, Maiden Fair'. What he did not have was an affinity for melodrama; while one can listen to his uncompromising exploitation of the melodic line in arias by Verdi and Puccini, one does not hear them in a theatrical context. In short, McCormack was not a Latin.

One might conclude that McCormack succeeded in front of an English audience only because, unlike their Italian counterparts, the English were susceptible to something less than the real thing. Exactly that was claimed for Melba, as Sir Thomas Beecham wrote in his autobiography, *A Mingled Chime*:

> In the maturer musical culture of the continent she had comparatively little success, her popularity being confined to England and those other Anglo-Saxon communities where the subtler and rarer sides of vocal talent are less valued.

To this, considering Melba's greatest successes were at Covent Garden, the same pen, in the same book, provides a delightful contradiction:

Margaret Burke-Sheridan (1889–1958) as Desdemona in Verdi's Otello. A theatrical temperament and a voluminous voice – in conjunction with good looks – made Sheridan a natural operatic heroine. She was greatly admired by both Puccini and Toscanini. The conductor on landing at Shannon Airport immediately enquired, 'Dov'e la Sheridan?' The extent of her popularity at La Scala and especially at the San Carlo Opera, Naples, was immense. On one occasion, when she was in mourning, the San Carlo closed down with the announcement: 'La Sheridan will not sing: her compatriot is dead.'

The audience of Covent Garden is, in my experience, and I have knowledge of nearly every important theatre of the world outside South America, the most critical as well as the best-informed on the subject of singing.

Perhaps it would be better to say that Anglo-Saxon and Latin ears hear with different temperaments; and for the most part, in London, McCormack's singing was not found to be lacking in temperament. Had he not been a newcomer, it is unlikely that *The Times* would have found his Turiddu 'vigorous'. But as a familiar performer, the same paper found that his singing of Elvino in *La Sonnambula* contained 'real pathos', while as Edgardo in *Lucia di Lammermoor*: 'he mourned her loss afterwards among the tombstones with proper intensity of feeling'; a role which the *Daily Telegraph* found the tenor sang with 'grace and fervour'. McCormack rarely failed to please in the lighter tenor roles. When he played Gerald in *Lakmé*, *The Times* regarded his singing as having been given with 'fine intensity of feeling'.

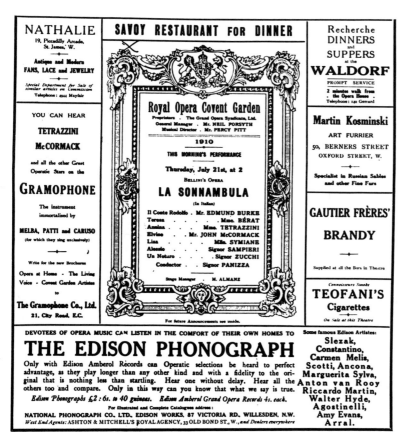

Covent Garden programme for *Sonnambula, 21 July 1910*. Elvino, common consent, was one of the roles which McCormack excelled. 'An admirable Elvino', wrote The Times in 19 'he sang not only with beautiful tone and perfect style of bel canto, but with amount of expression which it must be ho for any of the younger generation to fee On the left of the programme is advertisement for the Gramophone Cor pany, and below it an Edison advertiseme – fighting a rearguard action with impressive but unavailing cast list.

'Fine intensity of feeling' was not, however, a description that the press felt able to use regarding his acting. Rather the contrary. 'If only Mr McCormack's acting were as good as his singing, he would be a really great acquisition to the Covent Garden forces,' commented *The Graphic* in December 1907, and added: 'At present, however, his bearing on the stage is not calculated to carry complete conviction.' It probably never did. Only one review would suggest otherwise. When he appeared again as Turiddu, in 1908, *The Times* of 5 May wrote:

> In the first scene with Santuzza, especially, there is now purpose in all his movements; nothing is casual or uncertain, but every gesture, to the raising of an eyebrow, has its effect.

Thereafter *The Times* found fault frequently with his acting, which would suggest that the paper had over-reacted to what must have been, visually, a very disconcerting debut. By 11 May 1911 the paper was complaining after he had appeared as Rodolfo in *La Bohème* that:

> If he could only . . . learn to keep his arms still when there is nothing for them to do, one could easily forgive him his lack of dramatic power.

The *Illustrated London News* found exactly the same: 'He was found at times a little outside the picture, and he has still much to learn where appropriate gesture is concerned.'

But it was not in him to learn much about acting, perhaps not even the rudiments. In his last year at Covent Garden, by which time the tenor had been on the operatic stage for eight years, the *Illustrated London News*, 11 July 1914, could write of his Don Ottavio:

> . . . it was a great treat to hear him, but to watch his inconsequent movement and barren gesture was to lose a part of the pleasure that his voice provides.

Such comments suggest that less of McCormack is lost on wax than of some of his contemporaries. The voice and the stage performer never formed a unity. But the separation of eye from ear is an opera-goer's way of life. McCormack had to be judged by how he sounded, and he sounded like no one else. It was enough to make him a favourite tenor at Covent Garden.

The stars of the Edwardian opera – before time and Toscanini had relegated them to heaven – were primarily women. Melba reigned at Covent Garden as *prima donna assoluta*. But so great was the impact of the coloratura soprano Luisa Tetrazzini, who made her debut the month after McCormack, that the *Spectator* was prompted to head an article,

'The Re-Emergence of the Prima Donna'. The article went on to bemoan the fact (though hardly a new one so far as coloraturas were concerned) that audiences cared nothing for what opera was staged, provided only that Tetrazzini appeared in it. That made things easy for the management and difficult for everyone else. Outside the theatre, as reported by *The Graphic* of 23 November 1907:

> The congestion in Floral Street was . . . becoming a positive nuisance, and such was the competition among Tetrazzini-ites for the honour of being first in the field, that there seemed to be every possibility that, before long, they would be taking their breakfast there, as well as their lunch, tea and dinner.

Inside the theatre, such was the hysteria that Tetrazzini provoked that it was difficult, at least for a period, for anyone else in the cast to make much of a showing. In this context it was praise indeed for *The Times* of 4 May 1908 to write after a performance of *Lucia di Lammermoor*: 'It was well worth waiting until the final scene for Mr John McCormack's admirable singing of the famous tenor song.' *Punch*, 3 May 1911, went even further after a performance of *Lakmé*:

> I ask for nothing better than Mr McCormack's singing, and have certainly never heard anything half so good from a British officer in a lightish uniform.

Yet despite his prominence at Covent Garden, there lay a wide discrepancy between what McCormack sang on the opera stage and what he put on wax during the same period. Between 1906 and 1909 he recorded about ninety sides for the Odeon Company but only about fifteen were of operatic titles. This can be explained partly by the fact that when he began recording for Odeon in 1906 he was known only as a singer of ballads and songs. Prior to his opera debut, he recorded almost nothing but Irish ballads. He repeated for the Odeon Company much of what he had already done for the cylinder companies, whose reputations and beeswax were shortlived, and for the G & T Company, upon whose records of his immature art he was able to make considerable improvements. It is difficult to know precisely how many sides McCormack recorded before his Covent Garden debut because the Odeons were not numbered in strict chronological order. But if one subtracts the twenty-odd Odeons numbered below the 'Siciliana', LX 2488, his first operatic title, one is still left with a ratio of more than four to one against operatic titles, and removing the titles he duplicated does not significantly alter the ratio.

Luisa Tetrazzini (1871–1940), as sh[e] would have appeared when making he[r] Covent Garden debut as Violetta on [ ] November 1907. Three weeks later, on 2[ ] November, McCormack sang with her fo[r] the first time, taking the part of the Duke o[f] Mantua opposite her Gilda in a perfor[-]mance of Rigoletto.

Nor did the tenor, in any one year, ever record a preponderance of operatic titles. His first year with Victor, 1910, was the closest he came to it with half – twelve out of twenty-four sides – devoted to opera. The following year operatic titles dropped to a third; and after that, predictably, as his career turned increasingly away from opera, the inclusion of arias at his recording sessions became sporadic. Furthermore, the operatic excerpts McCormack recorded for Odeon were as much or more a reflection of what was current popular taste as what the tenor actually sang at Covent Garden. It is true that in 1908 he recorded 'Questa o quella' and 'La donna è mobile' from *Rigoletto*, 'Che gelida manina' from *La Bohème*, 'E lucevan le stelle' from *Tosca*, and appeared in all three operas. But only in the case of *Rigoletto* did the tenor sing the opera in the same year as he recorded arias from it. Rodolfo in *La Bohème* was to become one of his most frequently repeated roles, but he did not make his debut in the part until 1910, while his first performance as Cavaradossi did not take place until 1914. He recorded arias from *Mignon*, *L'Elisir d'Amore*, *Carmen* and even from *Pagliacci* and *Aida*: operas he never appeared in; while operas in which he did perform while his Odeon contract was still operative – *Don Giovanni*, *La Traviata*, *La Sonnambula* and *Lucia di Lammermoor* – were not represented in the Odeon catalogue at all.

As well as performing in opera, McCormack would have had the opportunity to sing the fifty-odd songs (and indeed the arias too) that he recorded for Odeon at the soirées and concerts which formed so substantial a part of Edwardian musical life; and very likely he did sing them all in public or private. The assembling of a record repertoire tended to be a haphazard affair in those days, but if the Odeon catalogue can be taken as reflecting the buying taste of the public, then it may be said that from the beginning the gramophone had anticipated where McCormack's true predilections lay.

Even as the tenor was beginning to lay the foundations of his operatic career, even before he had left his lodgings in Torrington Square for more affluent quarters on the strength of his Covent Garden debut, he was presented with his most famous encore. Perceval Graves recalled opening the door to Charles Marshall:

> ... who gave his name rather diffidently, with a request to meet McCormack who, luckily, happened to be at home, as he said: 'I have a song here which I think will suit him.' At that time Marshall was a struggling song-writer, a shade over fifty. Much encouraged by John's cordial reception, he sat down and played it over once and McCormack then sang it. After the first line, he

Punch *Cartoon, 6 May 1908, en⋯ Stars in Opposition, or the 'record' op⋯ duel. 'There is a popular superst⋯ wrote* The Graphic, *'to the effect ⋯ two* prima donne *cannot appear a⋯ same opera house without flying at ⋯ another's throats, sometimes metap⋯ cally, and sometimes literally.' And ha⋯ disposed of the superstition was abl⋯ assure its readers that 'there is no reas⋯ suppose ... that the rivalry between ⋯ Tetrazzini and Mme Melba wil⋯ anything but friendly, and certainly⋯ opportunity of contrasting their met⋯ should prove exceedingly interesting.'*

became enthusiastic. 'It's great. You must come with me at once to meet Mr Arthur Boosey. He is sure to take it.' And he did.

The song was 'I Hear You Calling Me', which McCormack introduced at a concert in Queen's Hall in 1908, and he scored an immmediate success with it. Thereafter, throughout his career, it remained to all intents and purposes the tenor's own property. Among his records, this song was by far and away his best seller. He recorded it twice for Odeon in 1908, and in 1910, 1911, 1921 and 1927 for the Victor Company in America. As with many of the items that he recorded for Odeon and later repeated, it is possible with this song to trace the development of his voice and vocal control, and more especially his development as a communicative artist. In the 1908 Odeon recordings of 'I Hear You Calling Me', there is a greater feel for words than in many of the other songs he recorded in the same year, yet it is evident that the singer is preoccupied with the vocal line. There is, moreover, an over-involvement with portamenti which diminishes the impact of the words. Two years later, the vocal line can be taken for granted, and the song gains meaning as we are made aware of the verbal content, especially the lines: 'Oh, the ringing gladness of your voice. . . . You spoke, do you remember? . . . Though years have stretched their weary lengths between. . . .' By 1921, the words are thrown into high relief, while the melodic line remains intact, but this recording is otherwise a disappointing one. McCormack's breathing is uncharacteristically heavy and the voice refuses to float.

It is in the 1927 version that we hear McCormack at the height of his powers. There is in this recording a dimension which is present in the Odeons, but used rather too obviously at that time: *a sense of timing*. That is to say, a pausing and pacing both verbal and melodic additional to the structure of the composition and made entirely for communicative purposes. It is strange that the art of timing should be universally recognized as being central to the actor's art but hardly spoken of in relation to the singer's. McCormack became a supreme exponent of it. In the two Odeons, for example, the final phrase, 'I hear you calling me', is laboured. The young singer is intent on ending with a climax. He achieves it, but without economy of means. The word 'I' is held fractionally too long; the word 'hear' is savoured, but with unnecessary emphasis. The pause between 'you' and 'calling' is longer than an audience requires to develop a sense of expectancy and the effect of the pianissimo which follows is diminished. In the 1927 version a small, almost imperceptible – a pregnant – pause divides 'you' and 'calling'. The singer rises on the phrase and we are neither ahead nor behind, but with him. He holds the sound and heightens the tension; release is implied, and the listener is expectant. We follow with ease the shapely and timely glide to earth on 'calling'. And with a subtle rhythmic emphasis on 'me', the phrase is concluded verbally and melodically. The immediacy of the contact McCormack had with his audiences, on record no less than in person, had much to do with his superb mastery of that element intuitive to all performing arts: *timing*.

Adelina Patti being greeted by Wil. Ganz on her arrival at Queen's Hall.

Victorians were made to last. It was in 1908 that McCormack had the opportunity to sing with a member of the *ancien régime*, Adelina Patti. A Diamond Jubilee Concert was held at Queen's Hall on 26 May 1908 to mark the fiftieth year in music of Wilhelm Ganz, a noted conductor of the time. Patti, who had had a long association with Ganz, once more came out of retirement and was, *The Graphic* declared:

> . . . the life and soul of the entertainment, singing several times, and afterwards kissing the hero of the day and crowning him with a laurel wreath.

Apart from singing, of course, 'Home, Sweet Home', Patti chose 'Voi che Sapete' from *The Marriage of Figaro*, Tosti's 'Serenata', Gounod's 'Serenade', and an eighteenth century song by Antonio Lotti, 'Pur Dicesti'.

The impression Patti made on the young McCormack, who sang 'Celeste Aida' on the same occasion, apparently ran deep. It is said that, after the concert, he went out and bought the Patti recording of 'Pur Dicesti', and then made a recording of it himself, with the quip: 'This will make the sopranos jealous.' No Odeon of 'Pur Dicesti' has, however, come to light, and the Victor recording made in 1923 is too late to fit the story, though not the quip. The record is exemplary for its tasteful embellishment, while McCormack maintains the inherent tension in the song with masterful discipline. I doubt if any modern soprano would have the technical resource to avoid 'swinging' the melody as successfully as McCormack. His coloratura runs show some hints of unease in the lower register; for example, in the first verse on the phrase 'Che fa tutto il mio piacer' sung to three triplets each preceded by an *acciaccatura*. This, no doubt, would offer little trouble to a soprano (or possibly to the tenor had his version been made even a few years earlier). Nevertheless, his recording compares favourably with Melba's (1910), in which the vocal lines are too straight, insufficiently 'rounded' to give the song its full measure of charm. And amongst male voices, the trills McCormack exhibits, so neatly attacked, so exquisitely blended with a turn into the natural vibrato of the voice at the end, would appear to belong to the past. Yet it is Patti's version, with its infectious sense of enjoyment, that is the most winning of the three.

It was also in 1908 that McCormack appeared in his first gala performance at Covent Garden. This one, held on 27 May 1908, was in honour of the French President, M. Fallières. Acts from *Faust* and *The Pearl Fishers* were given. McCormack sang with Tetrazzini, Sammarco and Marcoux in Act I of *I Pescatori*, which was given in Italian to facilitate the prima donna, if hardly to flatter the sensibilities of M. Fallières.

The press had little to say about what was to be seen or heard on stage, but little else was left to the imagination:

B<small>Y</small> COMMAND
OF
HIS MAJESTY THE KING
A
GALA PERFORMANCE
will be given on
WEDNESDAY, May 27,
at which
THEIR MAJESTIES
and
THE PRESIDENT of the FRENCH REPUBLIC
will be present.

The subscriptions on this evening will be suspended and transferred to Friday, July 31.

PROGRAMME.

I PESCATORI DI PERLE.

By Bizet. Act I.

Leila	Mme. TETRAZZINI.
Nadir	Mr. JOHN McCORMACK.
Zurga	Signor SAMMARCO.
Nurabad	Signor MARCOUX.

FAUST.

By Gounod. Act II. (Garden Scene).

Marguerite	Mme. MELBA.
Siebel	Miss HATCHARD.
Martha	Mme. EDNA THORNTON.
Faust	Signor ZENATELLO.
Mefistofele	M. JOURNET.

Conductor, Signor CAMPANINI.

PRICES :

Grand and Pit Tier Boxes	40 guineas each.
First Tier Boxes	30 guineas each.
Second Tier Boxes	15 guineas each.
Orchestra Stalls	7 guineas each.
Balcony Stalls	4 guineas each.

Amphitheatre Stalls all applied for.
Gallery (unreserved), 10s.

Applications should be made in writing to the General Manager, Mr. NEIL FORSYTH, and will be dealt with in strict priority.
Notice.—Doors open at 8. The public are requested to be seated at 9.

Advertisement from The Morning
*for the Gala performance at C
Garden in 1908. Those who con
about present-day prices of admission
opera could do worse than cast an e
these prices.*

Some twelve hours before the doors were opened the more determined of those who had hoped to secure seats had begun to collect, with camp-stools and other means of comfort for their long day of waiting. By eight o'clock, when the doors were opened, the crowd on the pavements of the troop-lined streets was dense, and a large number of police were busily engaged in keeping the approaches clear. . . .

ran an article in *The Times* (28 May), which maintained that:

. . . no anticipations could do justice to the lightness and grace of those broad bands and rippling festoons of roses which covered all

the tiers, beginning with pale pink at the proscenium and shading
gradually to the richest Royal crimson opposite the stage. . .

and estimated the number of blooms, a proportion of which had to be
artificial for fear the ladies might faint, at a quarter of a million. 'The
most brilliant feature . . . before the arrival of the Royal party,' *The Times*
thought, was to be found in 'the two boxes to the left of the grand tier.'
These were occupied by the Maharajah of Nepal and his suite:

> His Highness was wearing a headdress of incomparable
> splendour, a helmet composed entirely of diamonds and emeralds,
> and a bird of paradise and an osprey.

Others less conspicuous for their headdresses than for their place in
history could be named: Mr and Mrs Asquith, Sir Edward Grey, A. J.
Balfour and Mr Winston Churchill.

When it came to describing the fashion, *The Times* felt at a loss,
explaining that:

> When all the rank and fashion of England are collected into a
> comparatively small space and all in costumes worthy of the
> occasion, it is difficult to convey any impression of the effect on the
> eye. . . .

but made an attempt in the case of Lady Londonderry, 'whose tiara,
necklace and stomacher attracted all eyes to the Official and ex-official
box.' When it was known that the King had arrived, 'a whisper ran
through the house' and 'The King's Indian orderlies were seen to take
their places in the stalls.' The entire front entrance of the opera house was
reserved for the Royal party and had been adorned with accoutrements
of gold and crimson hangings, old French furniture, gilt mirrors and
quantities of palms. The performance began with the Marseillaise, and
eventually Tetrazzini, 'nobly supported' by McCormack, Sammarco
and Marcoux, opened the entertainment.

Heady days for the young tenor; Lily recalled:

> In the first flush of those Royal Opera days John was quite a
> 'dressy' young man, going to rehearsals in a silk hat, morning coat,
> and . . . white silk scarf.

Melba would not have approved of that. No more than McCormack
could have relished his first performance with Melba, and his first as
Rodolfo, when the 'diva' indicated that he was not supposed to take
curtain calls with her. A debut, moreover, which *The Musical Times*
thought had been taken with 'marked success'. And so began an uneasy

and sometimes frictional relationship. It did not, however, prevent Melba from inviting McCormack to be her leading tenor in the Melba-Williamson opera tour of Australia in 1911. The Melbourne correspondent of *The Times*, 5 April 1912, declared the tour to be:

> The most remarkable event that has yet occurred in Australian music . . . the houses being packed night after night, though prices were exactly three times those to which Australians were accustomed.

McCormack created an immediate impression. He made his debut as Alfredo opposite Melba's Violetta in a *Traviata* gala performance on 28 October 1911. The *Melbourne Herald* on 30 October found that it had made 'the acquaintance of a prepossessing young lyric tenor. A fresh and flexible voice, particularly rich in the upper register, used with pleasant ease. The same paper on 30 November did not appear to be unduly critical of his acting, for as the Duke of Mantua it was felt that his 'appearance and voice fully vindicated his claim to the position of a ducal lady-killer.' However, his performance in *Faust* prompted the *Herald* to write on 7 November: 'Into the puppet Faust, Mr McCormack failed to infuse any individuality. His nasal pronunciation of French was not to the advantage of his fine voice.'

The point regarding nasality is an interesting one because it was, and is, a criticism often made against McCormack. 'Sometimes he admitted', wrote Perceval Graves, 'to having recourse momentarily to *pincito*, or nasal production, when fatigued.' Yet the criticism would seem to arise from the associating of the tenor's vocal colour with nasal production. In fact, McCormack did not place his voice unusually high in the mask. The only example, it seems to me, among the tenor's records, barring his last, where the voice is patently placed in the nose, appears in the duet with Mario Sammarco 'All' idea di quel metallo' from *The Barber of Seville* (1911). On the coloratura run on the phrase 'Ah che d'amore' the tenor is briefly in difficulties and the voice leaps forward into the nose.

One may conclude with safety that Melba would not have extended an invitation to McCormack if she had felt his impact might have detracted from her own. A thought which, whatever it says about Melba, suggests McCormack was never impressive on stage. Likewise, having a light voice, he was not likely to outsing the prima donna, while his immaculate vocal production was a perfect match for Melba's. Not surprisingly, it was 'the consonance of the two beautiful voices' that the *Melbourne Herald* remarked upon when McCormack and Melba appeared in *Romeo and Juliet*.

Dame Nellie Melba as Violetta in Traviata, inscribed: 'To McCormack from his sincerely N Melba, 1909'. Melba made her debut Covent Garden in 1888 and bade farewell there thirty-eight years late 1926.

To Mrs. McCormack.
from his sincerely

To my dear friend Vincent Souvenir of
my first Romeo and of the autographs
MAY MOORE season with kindest regards &
wishes for New Year.
from his sincere friend
John McCormack

LEFT *Oscar Hammerstein (1847–1919) photographed in 1909, and* RIGHT *Cleofonte Campanini (1860–1919), the brother of the tenor Italo Campanini and the brother-in-law of Luisa Tetrazzini. He spent most of his life in America, but conducted at Covent Garden between 1904 and 1913. He conducted for McCormack in both England and America, and was one of the tenor's firmest admirers.*

LEFT McCormack as Romeo in Gounod's Romeo et Juliette. The inscription reads: 'To my dear friend Vincent [O'Brien] Souvenir of my first Romeo and of my Australian Season with kindest regard and wishes for New Year, from his sincere friend John McCormack, Sydney, 1911.'

The Australian opera tour was a useful foundation for the tenor's return visit, as a recitalist, in 1913. But two factors of much greater importance to McCormack's career were the influence of Luisa Tetrazzini and of the American impresario Oscar Hammerstein, who had set up his own opera house, the Manhattan, in 1906, in opposition to the mighty Metropolitan Opera. Having already made inroads into the box-office of the Metropolitan during two seasons, he went to London in 1909 to collect singers for his forthcoming autumn season. The story goes that he signed McCormack up during a rehearsal at Covent Garden with the remark: 'Don't you think an Irishman singing in Italian opera in New York is a cinch?' As neither the impresario nor the tenor were averse to good publicity the remark gained currency. But in an interview McCormack gave the *Musical Leader* in 1917 he said: 'Hammerstein kicked against my engagement. And this is how he objected: 'An Irish tenor in opera? I don't think so. . . .'

Hammerstein apparently took the advice of Luisa Tetrazzini, whose

impact at the Manhattan the previous season had been such as to travel back to England via the columns of *Punch*, as on 22 January 1908:

> The cheapest seats are five dollars each; first lap seats are ten dollars, and second lap, thirty. . . . On Wall Street such is the rage for opera and the great singer that men converse and carry on their business solely in recitative.

Certainly Tetrazzini did not doubt McCormack's abilities. She wrote in her autobiography, *My Life of Song*:

> My second season with Hammerstein was notable in one respect . . . when singing in London I had met John McCormack, the Irish tenor with the God-given voice. I found that his rich voice went so well with mine that I took him back with me to America . . . the Americans took John McCormack to their hearts, and the Irish tenor to America. . . .

Tetrazzini opened Hammerstein's autumn season on 10 November 1909 as Violetta in *La Traviata*, with McCormack as Alfredo and Sammarco as the father Germont. McCormack went down with 'flu

shortly before the performance, but went – literally – from his bed to the opera house. The *New York Herald* sub-headed its critique with: 'Physician always near', and 'Despite all he makes an excellent impression'. The paper found him: 'a broth of a boy. Twenty-seven years old with a robust frame and a pleasant face'; and noted that 'The audience liked him from the start.' Tetrazzini recalled:

> I was greatly pleased, as well as amused, when I read some of the newspaper accounts of his debut in New York. 'That McCormack is a decided acquisition to the company is undoubted', said the *New York Evening Post*. 'He is a pure lyric tenor, with a carefully trained voice; pure, clear, even and flexible, and naturally placed. His tones are always true and sympathetic, and his *mezza voce* was most effective. At the outset, in addition to his apparent physical suffering, he was palpably nervous, but Madame Tetrazzini came to his rescue by crossing the stage and giving him a gentle pat of encouragement'.

The Record of 8 December 1909 wrote humorously of the event:

> That Tetrazzini fully realizes his exceptional ability and delights in singing with him is evidenced in the persistent manner in which

she insists upon his assuming his burden of the applause. Last night Tetrazzini literally dragged the hero forth.

Five days later, McCormack appeared as Edgardo in *Lucia di Lammermoor* and 'deepened the impression he had made on his first appearance', according to the *New York Times*. The *New York Herald* concurred: 'All the pleasant things that have been said of the young Irish singer's voice may be repeated, with emphasis.' He could not put a foot wrong in New York. By the time he had sung Tonio in Donizetti's *La*

RIGHT *McCormack as Edgardo in L di Lammermoor.*

Manhattan Opera program January–March 1910.

Manhattan Opera House
West Thirty-fourth Street, Near Eighth Avenue.

Manhattan Grand Opera Company
SEASON 1909-1910

FOURTH SEASON OF GRAND OPERA
Under the Direction of
MR. OSCAR HAMMERSTEIN.

Saturday Afternoon, January 22, 1910, at 2 o'clock.

BOHEME
(In Italian.)

Opera in Four Acts, by PUCCINI.

MIMI, a Sewing Girl .... MME. CARMEN MELIS
MUSETTE, a Grisette .... MLLE. TRENTINI
RUDOLPH, a Poet .... MR. JOHN McCORMACK
MARCEL, a painter .... M. SAMMARCO
COLLINE, a Philosopher .... M. LASKIN
SCHAUNARD, a musician .... M. GILIBERT
BENOIT, a Landlord } .... M. DADDI
ALCINDORO, an Old Roue }
PARPIGNOL .... M. FRANZINI
CUSTOMS OFFICERS { .... M. FOSSETTA
.... M. ZURO

MUSICAL CONDUCTOR .... M. OSCAR ANSELMI
STAGE DIRECTOR .... M. JACQUES COINI

Manhattan Opera House
West Thirty-fourth Street, Near Eighth Avenue.

Manhattan Grand Opera Company
SEASON 1909-1910

FOURTH SEASON OF GRAND OPERA
Under the Direction of
MR. OSCAR HAMMERSTEIN.

Monday Evening, February 14, 1910, at 8 o'clock.

LA TRAVIATA
(In Italian.)

Opera in Four Acts, by VERDI.

VIOLETTA .... MME. TETRAZZINI
FLORA BERVOIX .... MISS ALICE GENTLE
ANNINA .... MLLE. SEVERINA
ALFREDO .... MR. JOHN McCORMACK
GERMONT, Father of Alfredo .... M. SAMMARCO
GASTON .... M. VENTURINI
BARON DUPHOL .... M. FOSSETTA
DOCTOR GRENVILLE .... M. DE GRAZIA
MARQUIS D'OBIGNY .... M. NEMO
GIUSEPPE .... M. PIERUCCI

MUSICAL CONDUCTOR .... M. OSCAR ANSELMI
STAGE DIRECTOR .... M. JACQUES COINI

Manhattan Opera House
West Thirty-fourth Street, Near Eighth Avenue.

Manhattan Grand Opera Company
SEASON 1909-1910

FOURTH SEASON OF GRAND OPERA
Under the Direction of
MR. OSCAR HAMMERSTEIN.

Wednesday Evening, March 2, 1910, at 8 o'clock.

Rigoletto
(In Italian.)

Opera in Four Acts, by VERDI.

GILDA .... MME. TETRAZZINI
MADDALENA .... MISS ALICE GENTLE
GIOVANNA .... MLLE. SEVERINA
THE COUNTESS OF CEPRANO .... MLLE. JOHNSTON
THE DUKE .... MR. JOHN McCORMACK
RIGOLETTO .... M. MAURICE RENAUD
SPARAFUCILE .... M. VALLIER
MONTERONE .... M. DE GRAZIA
MARULLO .... M. FOSSETTA
THE COUNT OF CEPRANO .... M. NEMO
BORSA .... M. VENTURINI
PAGE .... MLLE. KEENAN

MUSICAL CONDUCTOR........ M. OSCAR ANSELMI
STAGE DIRECTOR .... M. JACQUES COINI

CONTINUED ON NEXT PAGE

Manhattan Opera House
West Thirty-fourth Street, Near Eighth Avenue.

Manhattan Grand Opera Company
SEASON 1909-1910

FOURTH SEASON OF GRAND OPERA
Under the Direction of
MR. OSCAR HAMMERSTEIN.

Monday Evening, March 21, 1910, at 8 o'clock.

LAKME
(In Italian.)

An Opera in Three Acts, by LEO DELIBES.

LAKME .... MME. TETRAZZINI
MALIKA, a Slave .... MME. DUCHENE
ELLEN, Daughter of the British Governor,
.... MLLE. TRENTINI
ROSA, Her friend .... MLLE. VICARINO
MRS. BENSON, Governess .... MME. SEVERINA
GERALD, a British Officer ... MR. JOHN McCORMACK
FREDERICK, a British Officer .... M. CRABBE
NILIKANTHA, a Brahmin Priest, and father of
Lakme .... M. HUBERDEAU
HADJI, a Hindoo Slave .... M. RUSSO

MUSICAL CONDUCTOR .... M. CARLO NICOSIA
STAGE DIRECTOR .... M. JACQUES COINI

CONTINUED ON NEXT PAGE

*John and Lily – young marrieds. This ι
the kind of picture the tenor presented wh
he appeared in New York in 1909, an
carried tremendous appeal.*

Fille du Régiment on 22 November he was an established favourite. 'Mr McCormack was in splendid voice and proved himself even more of an artist than he has before, by his singing of the music allotted to Tonio', wrote the *New York Times*. The tenor aria in the second act, 'Per Viver Vicino a Maria', noted the *New York Herald*, 'was so admirably sung as to win some of the warmest applause of the evening. He had to repeat it.'

In 1910 Hammerstein was bought out by the Board of the Metropolitan Opera, who promptly formed the Philadelphia-Chicago Opera Company from Hammerstein's troopers. Under the auspices of the Metropolitan Board the company made forays from Chicago and Philadelphia into some of the larger American cities, and the cast made occasional guest appearances at the Metropolitan as well. So it was, on 29 November 1910, that McCormack made his Metropolitan debut in *La Traviata*, singing opposite Melba once again. Kreibel of the *New*

RIGHT *Portrait of Caruso, signed: ':
McCormack very friendly Enrico Carus
Boston, 1910'. Having heard the Italian f
the first time in London in 1904, t
twenty-year-old McCormack return
home bearing his photograph. On t
photograph appeared Caruso's autogra
and an inscription to McCorma
McCormack had written it himself. Whe
the two tenors were in Boston in 191
McCormack told this to Caruso, wh
finding the joke hugely amusing, whipp
up a photograph of himself, autographed
and presented it to McCormack.*

To McCormack
very friendly
Enrico Caruso
Boston 1910

*The Metropolitan Opera House, ~
York, c. 1900. Built in 1883, it ~
destroyed by fire nine years later ana
built on the same site. In 1966, it transf~
to the Lincoln Center for the perfor~
arts.*

York Times spoke of his 'delicate phrasing . . . the feeling and tenderness of his art'; while Henderson of *The Sun* found this tenderness made for 'a mild and inoffensive Alfredo'.

The following year McCormack created the role of Lieutenant Paul Merrill in the world premiere of *Natoma* by Victor Herbert. The opera was given first in Philadelphia on 25 February 1911 and then transferred to the Metropolitan three days later. The librettist, J. D. Redding, was an American; and Victor Herbert, although born in Ireland and educated in Germany, had lived in America for more than twenty years. So *Natoma* – the story of an Indian girl – was deemed to be an all﹍ American opera. The interest in the opera was immense, as was the cost, a state of affairs which produced an anguished cry from the American correspondent of *The Times* on 11 March:

> We are a wealthy nation, and when we set out to do a thing we do not spare expense. No expense has been spared in the production of *Natoma* in orchestra, singers, setting, or advertising. The only drawback to the brilliancy of the occasion was that scarcely a gleam of genuine art, of the art that is playful in spirit and indifferent to its wage, had gone into the making of the work. Consequently, there was nothing to lift the audience from an enthusiasm which was after all only amiable and patriotic to the plane of genuine artistic emotion. That unfortunately, cannot be

erbert (1859–1924). At top the
wrote: 'To my dear friends Mr and
McCormack with all good wishes,
rbert, April, 1911.' Below: 'And
nks to you dear John for your fine
d your neverending enthusiasm for a
ishman's effort.' On the left of the
re themes from Natoma. Herbert
eved the same success with his two
atoma and Madeleine that he did
perettas. Naughty Marietta was
ed at the same time as Natoma and
ry much more popular. McCormack
'm falling in love with someone' from
 Marietta in March 1911, but did
 'Paul's address' from Natoma until
the following year.

tonight. Shall we ever be really musical until we give up trying to
buy it?

'My whole conception of opera,' Herbert had told the New York Times
(22 January 1911), 'is that it should be based on melody' – but nothing
in Natoma was memorable. 'We want to show that an opera can be sung
in English,' said J. D. Redding on the same occasion, but H. E. Kreibel
described the lyrics as the 'merest doggerel'. And they were by no means
easy to sing. As The Times critic commented: 'Several of the principals,
notably Mr John McCormack, Mr Mario Sammarco, Miss Lillian
Grenville, and somewhat less markedly, Miss Mary Garden, in the title
role, might as well have been singing in Italian.' Mary Garden, for
whom the role of Natoma had been written, acquitted herself with
distinction. 'She has sacrificed remorselessly everything to the make-up
of the Indian,' wrote the New York Times, 'and in mask and coiffure, as
well as in costume, she has put herself entirely into the character. The
music lies very well for her voice, and she sings it as well as she does any
music.' The same paper found that: 'Mr John McCormack sings the
music of the American naval officer admirably and he makes an earnest
effort to embody the part, in which his lack of dramatic temperament
and skill stands somewhat in his way.' Irving Kolodin, in The Story of
The Metropolitan Opera, put it rather differently: 'McCormack's
Lieutenant Paul Merrill was not merely as bad as the role: it was worse.'

McCormack did not sing again at the Metropolitan, in opera, until the 1917–18 season. When he reappeared as Rodolfo in *La Bohème* opinion was divided. The *New York Times* of 17 November 1917 thought the part: 'not one best adapted for him. It needs a livelier dramatic temperament than his, a potency of more passionate expression . . .' but admitted that his singing was: 'of its kind unsurpassable, in quality of tone, in purity of diction, in finish of phrase. . . .' *The Sun*, on the other hand, thought his singing 'excellently suited' to the music; but found him as Pinkerton in *Madame Butterfly*: 'inconceivable as a whale-boat officer, [though] he sang the music surpassingly well.' McCormack's last appearance in opera in America was in *Butterfly* in New York. More notable was his Cavaradossi sung to Geraldine Farrar's Tosca, on 20 February 1918. 'Dramatically, Mr McCormack is not an ideal Mario', was the predictable comment of the *New York Herald*, but the *New York Times* of 21 February noted:

> Mr McCormack earned an ovation after Cavaradossi's air in the closing act, which he sang quietly seated at the prisoner's table. . . . The Irish Tenor has not been in better form in any opera, either during his occasional Metropolitan appearances this season, or years ago at the Manhattan.

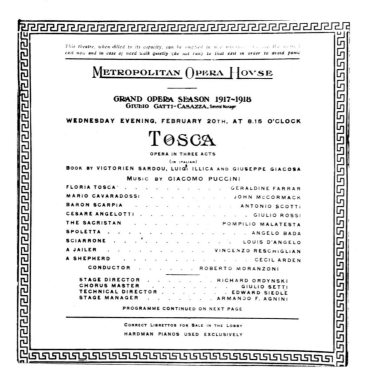

RIGHT *McCormack as Mario Cavaradoss Tosca. 'In his cape coat and top boots as revolutionist of the torture scene, he borrow something of lively romance from famous her in "The Highwayman" or "The Shaughrau with no harm to Puccini or Sardou.' (Ne York Times, 21 February 1918)*

LEFT *Programme for* Tosca, *Metropoli Opera, 20 February 1918. The crit preferred McCormack's singing in the smal Manhattan Opera House, but his perfect fo of tone enabled him to be heard with ease even the upper reaches of the Metropolitan. Aft this performance of* Tosca, *the New Yo* Herald *critic noted: 'His enunciation was cl enough to arouse envy in many an Itali singer.'*

Puccini operas all, but no Mozart. McCormack never sang in *Don Giovanni* at the Metropolitan for the simple reason that the opera was not staged there at all between 1907 and 1935. But outside the Metropolitan he did sing the role of Don Ottavio, and as a Mozartian was generally regarded, certainly among male voices, as without a rival: 'Mozart wrote for just such a voice and singer as John McCormack,' was a typical commentary following an appearance as Don Ottavio, 'and those long sustained phrases were of perfect beauty as he sang them, sounding so natural and spontaneous that for the moment you almost forgot the art that made them possible. . . . ['Il Mio Tesoro'] was so beautifully done that after he had bowed before the curtain several times, Mr Campanini had him stand there and repeat it.' Felix Weingartner showed less restraint than Campanini. On one occasion after 'Il Mio Tesoro' he laid down his baton and led the applause.

The administration of the Metropolitan Opera believed, apparently, that a sufficiently strong cast could not be assembled for *Don Giovanni*. The great German soprano Lily Lehmann expected to do well enough

The Polish tenor Jean de Resz[ke] [with] McCormack photographed outs[ide] Pole's villa at Nice, 1921. McC[ormack] sang for de Reszke's pupils. [In the] twenties, McCormack may well h[ave felt] that he belonged to a vanishing b[reed of] vocalists. In a private letter from [...] C. Wagner, dated 6 December 1[9..] wrote: 'Look out for tenor called [...] hell of a good voice, but sings like a [...] nuff sed! However is interesting.'

in 1914 at the Mozarteum, Salzburg, with a cast headed by herself as Donna Anna, and which included Geraldine Farrar as Zerlina, McCormack as Don Ottavio and Andreas de Segurola as the Don. The invitation was an honour McCormack cherished, but the production never took place. Even as the tenor was travelling to Austria via Belgium, news came to him that the First World War had begun, and he returned to the States.

It was, however, in Europe that McCormack sang in his final operas: at Monte Carlo in the 1923 season, when he appeared in *The Barber of Seville*, *Madame Butterfly*, *Tosca*, *Martha*; and finally in Mussorgsky's *La Foire de Sorotchintzi* he created the role of Gritzko in the world premiere performed on 17 March 1923, making his last operatic appearance in the same role on 25 March. He was not yet forty. At the end of his opera days, McCormack could say with much candour and little hyperbole: 'I was the world's worst actor', implying that opera was not, therefore, his true metier. But is it really necessary to be an actor in order to be an opera singer?

...amme for La Foire de Sorot- ...zi, Opéra de Monte-Carlo, 17 ...a 1923. McCormack created the role ...itzko in the world premiere of this ... It is sometimes thought that Monte ... lacked first-rate tenors in this period. ...was far from being the case. Among ...nors, there was the Belgian Fernand ...eau; the American, Charles Hac- ... and even the Russian Dmitri ...nov. Why the Russian did not create ...le of Gritzko is not known.

'I am the world's worst actor.... Th
a few operatic roles that I enjoy p
My favourite is Rodolfo in La Boh
He's a real fellow. I can sing him a
feel like a human being. I can pace
down the stage, with my hands
trouser pockets, and seem true to cha
(From an interview in The Green
Magazine.)

3 THE RECITALIST

For an opera singer, even a great one, an ability to act is a gratuitous accomplishment, not a necessity. Melba is an obvious example. 'She sang exquisitely, but in our opinion was never Desdemona for five minutes on end', wrote the *Illustrated London News* (11 July 1908) after a performance of *Otello*. That was the general opinion of the prima donna – that she remained Melba, whatever and whenever she sang. Even Giovanni Zenatello, who became one of the most famous of Otellos, was judged, in the same performance 'not to look the part'.

In McCormack's time, much more than in our own, realism was a secondary consideration, or of no consideration at all. 'Last night Madame Tetrazzini's costumes were half a century ahead of everyone else's in the play,' wrote *The London Times'* critic on 1 May 1908, after a performance of *La Traviata*, and added: 'Let us hope she is still open to correction.' The hope was in vain. And considering that Tetrazzini, at the height of her powers, weighed in at around fifteen stone – and she was far from being a tall woman – clothes contemporary with what the rest of the cast were wearing would hardly have done much to create the illusion of a consumptive. Most of the cast were in need of correction after a performance of *La Traviata* in 1911, when 'The style of the costumes covered a wide range, from the crinoline period to that of about 1908.' When the Russian soprano Félia Litvinne assumed the role of Aida in 1907 *The Graphic* of 26 October, in common with other periodicals, felt that no one:

> could possibly have taken her for the daughter of that splendid artist, Sig. Sammarco, for Amonasro's complexion was aggressively Ethiopian, while that of Aida was of the tint known to *modistes* as pale biscuit. Perhaps, however, Mme Litvinne has

Punch *cartoon of Litvinne as Aid*
Sammarco as Amonasro (23 O
1907) – the shading tells the tale.

unearthed some interesting record of the part which proves Aida's mother was an albino.

In this milieu, why should McCormack's lack of acting ability have mattered? The short answer is that it did not matter, if one is using the term acting in its most basic sense of being the ability to assume and project a character other than one's own. Few actors and fewer singers, it seems to me, actually do that. The vast majority, in either case, while projecting some elements of each character assumed, exhibit the selfsame personality in each; and in the Edwardian opera, one may be certain, McCormack was not alone in having, as *The Times* put it: 'the same vocal methods and the same gestures to suit all occasions'. There is, however, another and probably more prevalent sense in which the term acting is used, or misused. Since character portrayal is a representational art, it implies fidelity to a blueprint or to criteria that are external to the performance and to the opera house; but a performer may also be judged 'credible' or 'convincing' simply on account of the manner in which he performs, without reference to anything outside or beyond the performance itself. It is then not so much a question of whether the audience believes in a character so much as whether they believe in the performer. Tetrazzini understood this well, when in an interview with the *Daily Express* on 10 March 1929 she said:

> You may have the voice of an angel, and have it trained by a maestro who is a demi-god, but unless you are gifted with a personality which gives equal pleasure to your audience, you will never become popular or famous. . . . Naturally, I have always taken care to put personality into my work.

RIGHT *Enrico Caruso as Rhadame*
Aida. An affinity for the stage
derives from the fact that a stage role o
the performer a mask. This was appare
the case with Caruso. Charles L. Wa
wrote: 'One day I mentioned concerts
it startled him. "Never!" he cried. "I
for the opera – in costume I am in chara
and comfortable; in a dress suit – u
would I do with my hands?" W
several years later, Coppicus [an
presario] offered him double and triple
like a good foreigner he soon found out u
to do with his hands – he held them o
Caruso always was ill at ease on the con
platform. He would take a dozen songs
the piano on each appearance scheduled
the programme. After each one, he wo
look around, measure the distance to
wings, and then sing another song. .
seemed to be worried as to how to get on a
off stage. Many times he would sing six
eight songs to a group, so as to obviate
necessity of making those dreaded entran
and exits.' By comparison, wh
McCormack appeared in opera, he lost
own sense of identity and could not add
that of the character.

The Great Irish Tenor

In the opera house, Tetrazzini was no more than herself. Or to be more precise, she acted no more than intermittently (and I suspect this was a generally accepted practice at the time). Writing of her first performance in *La Traviata* at the Manhattan in 1909 the *New York Times* noted that in the first act: 'She threw a kiss to the audience as she entered.' That was not all. She was apt to acknowledge, with a wink or a wave, people she could recognize in the audience; and to join the audience in applause for another performer. Not surprisingly, the *New York Times* formed the opinion that: 'Much that she does cannot meet with serious approval.' This was certainly not acting as it is generally understood, but audiences loved it; and whatever one may call it, the fact remains that Tetrazzini knew how to make the theatre work for her.

McCormack did not. Asked for an opinion of Melba's acting, or lack of it, the tenor replied: 'She was just about as good or as bad as myself.' That was probably fair comment so far as characterization was concerned. But Melba knew how to move on stage; she had a regal deportment which, if not evocative of Mimi or Marguerite, appealed to contemporary audiences, and was indeed part of the fashion of the times.

McCormack's instincts were not really of the theatre. Clothed with an opera role, his personality was muted. 'I never felt at ease in opera', he confessed, and it showed. On stage he lacked credibility. By comparison, on the concert platform, by himself, as himself, McCormack exhibited a rare authenticity. His pesonality seemed to be quite free of superimpositions, or those he had were patently transparent. On the platform or off, his responses were first responses. He seemed to combine the imaginative capacity of childhood with the mature musical judgement of adulthood. Whatever he sang, he had the knack of making his suspension of disbelief absolute and a genius for transmitting it. In *High-Fidelity* magazine of February 1957 the American critic Max de Schauensee provides an evocative pen-sketch of the recitalist:

> When I think of the word 'singer', stripped of any extraneous dramatic connotations and in its purest sense, I see John McCormack standing on the concert platform – his head thrown back, his eyes closed, in his hands the little black book he always carried, open, but never glanced at, as he wove a spell over his completely hushed listeners. John McCormack was truly a singer for the people; he was also a singer's singer.

> When John McCormack sang, he aroused a variety of impressions that soon blended into a warm genial sensation of relaxed contentment. He was a completely manly singer, though

From the concert sequence of Song O' My Heart. *Note the little black book in the tenor's hands.*

distinctly not of that breed of he-man vocalists who are best served by such fare as 'Give a man a pipe he can smoke; give a man a horse he can ride' (accompanied by pugilistic flailings at the surrounding air). He did not exploit masculinity, but there was never any doubt that here stood a romantic hero whose song could make the fair sex swoon. Also present, and paradoxically so, was a schoolboy type of purity – I don't know what else to call it – that had its special appeal and that could stir in any sensitive adult a nostalgic regret for his own lost youth.

Without doubt, he was one of the truly remakable personalities among musicians active in the first half of the twentieth century. Perhaps the three who were able to reach the heart most directly were Paderewski, Kreisler, and McCormack, and of them, McCormack was very probably the surest technician. Like Caruso, he had a forthright charm that, free of any complications, made its effect with a minimum of time and effort. People who listened to McCormack were drawn to him. Let us call this personal magnetism. We are apt to refer to people we are drawn to as 'warm' or 'genuine'; McCormack was just that. Even when he was singing in a huge auditorium, he always gave me the sensation of person-to-person intimacy.

McCormack could achieve little of this in the opera house. Henry Pleasants in *The Great Singers* suggests why:

> It was this knack, possibly stemming from a predilection to talk, to be listened to, and to convince, that predestined him for the recital hall. He was, in private life, gregarious, garrulous and disputatious, with a penchant for holding forth on any and all subjects. In the recital hall he had, of course, a captive audience, and he relished it. This was his natural habitat.

The youthful celebrity. Women preponderated at his concerts.

Another clue is, perhaps, to be found in a radio broadcast the tenor made with Bing Crosby in the mid-thirties. Crosby immediately established his usual easy relationship. McCormack, who could so readily put across a feeling of ease in the concert hall, could not do so in this context. He was not short of radio experience by this time, but he comes across as being uncomfortable. In opera, he generated little rapport with his prima donnas; and much the same could be said about his film *Song O' My Heart*, since he does not establish convincing relationships with the rest of the cast. There may have been elements of self-doubt embedded in his personality which he could not reconcile with the presence of other performers; he could be a very scathing critic and colleague when in the mood. As a performer, McCormack was most effective on his own; and indeed it seems that he had to be on his own to be effective.

The actor, in whatever way else he may equip himself, must to some extent travel the road that ends in the mental state Mary Garden described in her autobiography. She did not *act* her parts, she *became* them. McCormack, it seems to me, was incapable of just that kind of mental process. And what was, at best, no disadvantage on the opera stage, became an inestimable virtue on the concert platform. Compton Mackenzie was claiming nothing very controversial when he wrote in *The Gramophone* in 1924: 'It is the capacity for *being* the song he is singing that gives him the right to be called the world's greatest living tenor.' But Mackenzie pursues this analysis of McCormack's commitment to what he sang in a way which seems very wide of the mark:

> I heard him in Dublin sing a song about a fairy behind a hedge...
> and by the intensity with which he was being that fairy, he
> bewitched his audience.

McCormack never *became* any of the characters he sang about. He might just as well have become Rodolfo in *La Bohème* or Cavaradossi in *Tosca* as a fairy. Commitment and identification are not the same thing. Songs provided him with two choices: to sing in the first person or in the third, but in either case he sang as himself. He equated the art of song with the art of narrative – or story telling – as has so often been said. This was especially true of his singing of Irish ballads. The intimacy with which he sang these songs brought with it the sense that he was confiding in his audience: the pathetic situation of Terence being left to his small town life by Kathleen in the song 'Terence's Farewell to Kathleen'; the whimsical dreams of the emigrant bound for the New World and at the same time torn by leaving home in 'Off to Philadelphia'; or the confession of love for the maid with the nut brown hair in 'The Star of the County Down'. And few things appeal to human nature so much as being the recipient of confidences. Moreover, McCormack seemed to have solved the problem of addressing the subject or object in any particular song at the same time as addressing his audience. There was no apparent ambivalence in his address. His art was the art of reported speech. It was an unusual, almost an unique art.

By comparison with the Irish recitalist, the singers of the nineteenth century must have appeared as remote figures to all but an elite circle. The desire by the public at large for closer contact with the 'divi' and 'dive' of the opera was reflected in the increasing newspaper publicity given to singers, but the cadre of the opera became intangible and irrelevant to the social needs in this century. The recital offered a more personalized formula, and McCormack exploited it.

His concert career began in earnest in 1912, an appropriate time, as the gramophone reveals. Just two years earlier, the Victor Talking Machine Company bought out his Odeon contract, which still had a year to run. The year 1910 marks a milestone in the McCormack discography – 1910 divides the past from the future tenor. In that year he reached maturity as a performer. Old timers, those who still remain, will tell you that McCormack's singing during his early years had a quality that he lost later. A comparison between the Odeons and the first Victors reveal what they mean. On those early Odeons, McCormack sings for himself. We listen as spectators, rather than as members of an audience. Our presence is unknown: we are onlookers. In 'Come Back to Erin', the tenor jaunts along in simple innocence. Each verse sounds similar. The diction has improved from the early G & Ts, but the rounded vowels are, for the most part, still to come. The tenor, interestingly, sounds more secure in Italian arias and Italian songs: 'E Lucevan le Stelle'; 'Che Gelida Manina'; 'Questa o Quella'; 'Lolita' (especially the piano version) and the 'Siciliana' (in an English translation) than in English songs. The reason may have been that in regarding himself as an opera singer McCormack was oriented towards the more expansive style inherent in Italian composition. On the Odeon label he sings 'I Hear You Calling Me' more operatically than he would do later. He sings *forte* on the word 'calling' in the introductory line and on the insignificant word 'of' in the phrase 'distant music of your voice', when the rest of the phrase is given *mezza voce*. The operatic effect of this would have been more apparent in the concert hall than it is on record, on account of the fact that recording condenses dynamic contrasts.

There is a strong sense of verve, and of a sheer youthful joy in music-making on these early records, something akin to the autointoxication beloved of Italians. This works well for the tenor in, for example, 'Che Gelida Manina' and 'Lolita', but not in 'The Flower Song' from *Carmen*. Here, McCormack begins quietly enough and with self-possession, but by the time he has reached the middle of the aria, he has become engrossed in his own emotions, and the listener is left outside. One is conscious too of how closely, even dutifully, McCormack marked the beat of the music during this period, as in 'Oft in the Stilly Night' and 'Terence's Farewell to Kathleen'. It circumscribes his evident verbal awareness. The preoccupation is with the vocal line, and the effects he achieves are made mainly through the music and not so much through the words. He uses frequently and with brilliant clarity such devices as mordents, turns and appoggiaturas. Significantly, he

*tenor with his family in
Francisco, 1912. He
ected an ideal of Irish-
erican manhood.*

later omitted many of these ornaments in order to make the verbal meaning of phrases more apparent.

One senses that from 1910 onwards the tenor's sheer pleasure in the act of singing has been replaced by a new impetus: singing as a communicative process. The progression of this change is evident in some 1909 Odeons, such as 'Celeste Aida' and the finely controlled 'Spirto gentil'. It was startlingly complete by 1910. On all those twenty-four Victor sides McCormack establishes immediate contact with his unseen audience, and maintains it unerringly. As in 'Fra poco ricovero' and 'Una furtiva lagrima', he now shapes and moulds each phrase, giving each exquisite form, holding each phrase up to view. Here is open throated singing at its most lovely. All the tenor does is now done purposefully, yet spontaneity continues to pervade his entire craft. There is a new sense of confidence in new-found powers in the caressive 'Per viver vicino a Maria' and the effortless 'Salve, dimora', where the top C is taken on the 'u' vowel in 'fanciulla' as written, not on the 'la' as is common practice. And *the sense of timing* in 'Tu che a Dio spiegasti l'ali' is certainly not matched by anything that had come before.

When the Victor Company bought out the Odeon contract for £2,000 Victor's sister company in England, His Master's Voice, then The Gramophone Company, was invited to share in the deal, but refused. At the time the company could boast of having such continental tenors as Enrico Caruso, Leo Slezak, Francesco Tamagno, Fernando de Lucia, as well as several English operatic tenors. To this list, they could apparently find little reason for adding an Irish tenor. That McCormack might have an alternative potential as a concert artist did not seem to weigh with them either. Despite the prominence he had achieved in English recital halls, the company may have been put off by his brogue as certain members of the press had been and may have felt his appeal would be limited. And there could have been a more important reason. Only one British artist had achieved international recognition *and* become a best selling record artist, simply through oratorio and concert appearances, and she seemed exceptional in every way. That was Clara Butt.

But the Americans knew better or, at least, three that counted did: Oscar Hammerstein, Calvin Child of the Victor Company, and the impresario Charles L. Wagner. Hammerstein impressed on the tenor his belief that his true métier lay in recital, Calvin Child organized the transfer deal with Odeon, and Wagner made McCormack's concert career a practical reality. 'I knew that John had been increasingly keen to leave opera and give concerts only', Lily commented in *I Hear You Calling Me*, referring to the period shortly after the tenor had made his

TESTIMONI

18th May, 1910

I believe that the process by which my new Gramophone Records are made is the most perfect of all methods of voice reproduction, and I consider that these records alone, as made by your process, are absolutely perfect reproductions of my voice.

Yours very truly,

John McCormack

The Gramophone Co. Ltd.,
21, City Road,
London, E.C.

Gramophone Company advertiser 1910. Reluctant though the Gramo[phone] Company had been to support the V[ictor] Company in buying out McCorm[ack's] Odeon contract, they reacted with ala[crity] when it came to advertising the tenor.

operatic debut in the States. There was every reason to believe that such a course was possible. The first American concert in which he participated took place at the Manhattan Opera House on 18 November 1909. His impact on that occasion may be gauged from the fact that when Hammerstein advertised his next concert, for 11 December, McCormack was given top billing, and bracketed after his name as an added incentive was the announcement that 'He will sing "The Snowy Breasted Pearl".' The *New York Herald* of 13 December commented:

> Of the singers, Mr John McCormack pleased the audience greatly with his Irish ballads, as he had done previously in the same place. Of course, he had to add to the programme in response to the plaudits.

McCormack's initial contract with Wagner was drawn up in January 1910. It was for only five weeks and was not to begin until September 1912. At the time when McCormack was approached by Wagner he was under contract to the Chicago-Philadelphia Opera Company, who had an option of re-contracting him until February 1912. Wagner's concert tour was intended to take place just before the opera season, and in the event of the opera company not taking up its options, it was to be extended from five to twenty weeks. This was in fact what happened, and McCormack remained in partnership with Wagner until 1924.

The Chicago-Philadelphia Opera Company had an arrangement with the Wolfsohn Bureau whereby McCormack was to sing thirty-four concerts in the spring of 1912. Wagner observed the way the tenor was being handled during these months with disapproval. He wrote in his autobiography, *Seeing Stars*:

es L. Wagner.

> He had been badly managed, both as to his concert appearances under the opera contract and under this farmed-out management. In the first case, on one tour he was sent out with five other singers, all more or less known in grand opera and called the International Company. McCormack himself, who was outstanding in the group, was not properly exploited.
>
> These early managers emphasised his nationality – an unnecessary tactic. John McCormack never belonged solely to the Irish race; he belonged to the entire musical world. . . . During the 34-date Wolfsohn-Quinlan tour, they announced him with green ink and heralded an *Irish ballad singer*. I came to the conclusion when I noted these maneouvers that shamrocks were no more necessary in exploiting McCormack than carving a polar bear on an ice pitcher. . . .

I stayed with John most of the time he was making the Wolfsohn-Quinlan tour so was able to gauge the effects of these improper managerial moves. . . .

Business was only fair *en tour*. It looked as though the local managers felt this tenor was good for only one appearance, but I was sure I knew better; that the poor houses were caused by poor management. I had reason to make these close studies of my golden-voiced artist. My entire fortune was tied up in his future. . .

There can be no question that had McCormack not been Irish, and had he not sung Irish ballads, his popularity would not have reached the sensational heights that it did. Nevertheless, Wagner may well have been right, that to *introduce* McCormack as an 'Irish ballad singer' was automatically to deprive him of a certain status, a status likely to be reflected at the box-office. In other words, it was one thing to go to hear a recitalist, albeit untried, who sang ballads; it was quite another to go to hear a ballad singer. Wagner served McCormack well; again in *Seeing Stars* he wrote:

Always I have contended that it is not solely the artist who draws. The exploitation of his artistry is equally as important. Americans are so busy that they need to be reminded again and again. Even when our houses sold out, our advertising continued, for everyone turned away at the box office probably told a dozen friends that that was the *one* thing he had wanted to hear all season. The public always craves that which is hard to get.

In his first season with Wagner, the tenor sang sixty-seven concerts and appeared in twelve opera performances. He soon averaged a concert appearance every other day over a six or eight month period. With no air travel, cities had to be joined by train and car travel; and more often than not there was extensive travelling between each concert. His reputation as a concert platform singer gathered impetus immediately and a division between the opera singer and the recitalist began to emerge. Between 1914 and 1918, when the tenor sang in opera in America for the last time, he appeared in only nine opera performances. In the same period, he gave something like four hundred concerts. His 1914–15 season contained his most intensive schedule: ninety-five concerts, a schedule his wife made certain was not repeated for fear of the toll on his health.

It would be difficult to deny that McCormack answered some immediate need in America. He was a phenomenon of the times. How else to describe the audience response wherever he sang? Newsclips of the day tell the tale: 'McCormack's Fifth Greater New York Recital of

Letter from McCormack in Hutc[h] Kansas, to Charles L. Wagner, u[n] The strain involved in constant tou[r] well portrayed in this letter. The ten[or] rarely restrained when it came to givi[ng] to his feelings. In another letter to W[agner] dated 25 October 1919, from Ames, McCormack began: 'Dear Ch[arles] May God forgive you for putting me [in the] most superjerk water town, for I neve[r]

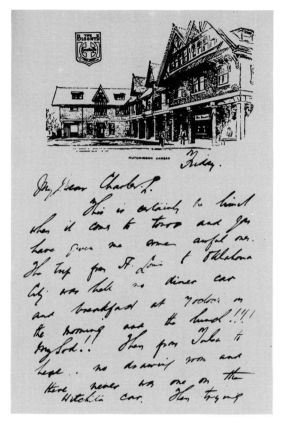

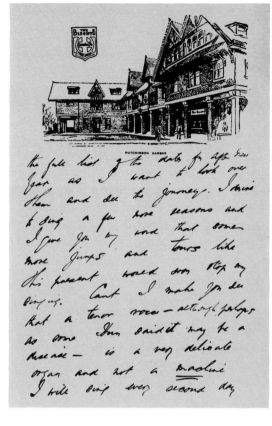

Friday.

My dear Charles L.

This is certainly the limit when it comes to travel and you have given me some awful ones. The trip from St. Louis to Oklahoma City was hell — no diner car and breakfast at 10 o'clock in the morning and the lunch!!! my God!! Then from Tulsa to here — no drawing room and there never was one on the Hutchin car. Then trying

the full list of the dates for after New Year as I want to look over them and see the journeys. I want to sing a few more seasons and I give you my word that some more jumps and tours like this present would soon stop my singing. Cant I make you see that a tenor voice — although perhaps as some one [?] said it may be a machine — is a very delicate organ and not a <u>machine</u> I will sing every second day

to snatch a sandwich in a station after a hard concert, then two and half hours in trolley car. Now Charles this wont suit me it may be all right for a Chatauqua troupe but not for mine. Of course you may blame the Railroad Administration, but you must not make your journeys harder when the Railroad accommodation gets worse. That is not the way things are done. I notice also that I arrive Lincoln the noon of the day of the Concert, this is monstrous not fair, to me or the public and I hereby give notice if there is not a drawing room to Lincoln, there will be <u>no</u> concert as I will go direct to Chicago. When you come there please bring

for eight months if you do not give a journey of more than eight hours between, I am not getting younger I am sorry to say and if you wont take my voice into consideration I will just have to do so myself and in our next contract (if any) put a clause in that the towns and dates be sent up to me for my O.K. Now a last word of advice dont write me a smart letter that you can say "that ought to hold John for a while." Two of us can do that and I'll back myself. Just give this your sympathetic attention it is not meant as a kick it is just a protest (subtle difference) from a very tired tenor.

Regards yours John McCormack

Season – huge audience seems insatiate'; 'McCormack furore in San Francisco – great tenor attracts clamoring throngs'; 'St Paul box-office records broken'; 'Record Richmond audience greets McCormack, return engagement of Irish tenor'. These clips are typical. In any part of the States, by the middle war years, McCormack could fill any auditorium in any city. But few auditoria, even the largest, could accommodate the numbers he attracted. In Boston, he could appear four times in the space of a week, and did so several seasons running. In New York, he could fill Carnegie Hall to over capacity up to ten times in a single season. The *Musical Courier* of 20 January 1916 commented:

> If one were to judge from the crowds that frantically endeavoured to get into the building, filling every box and seat in the house, overflowing on to the stage, and occupying every bit of standing room which the fire laws permitted, said judge would undoubtedly have concluded that the celebrated Irish tenor was about to retire and might never sing again in public; while on the contrary, he is announced for another appearance in the same hall on February 13.

McCormack concert at the New Hippodrome, 28 April 1918, which h audience of 7000, divided as follows: seated in the auditorium, 1000 seated b the tenor and 1000 standing. 'I McCormack,' wrote Wagner in Se Stars, 'we established the New Hippodrome as a Sunday concert ha that great year of 1915. We played Joh many as nine times in one season an concerts are what established the succe this popular venture.' The Hippod was pulled down in 1939.

In Carnegie Hall, the Hippodrome or the Metropolitan Opera House, the scenes were the same, and the tenor moved from one to the other during the same season. Seats on stage, even in the largest auditoria, became the rule. *Phil. N. American* 29 April 1916:

> John McCormack's third recital of this season at the Metropolitan Opera House last night was attended by nearly 5,000 persons. [It was] probably the largest audience ever attracted to that big auditorium. Not only was every seat in the house occupied, but 500 chairs on the stage and 300 chairs in the orchestra pit were filled before the concert began. And lining the brass rails at the rear of the parquet were several hundred standees.

Max de Schauensee has written: 'McCormack . . . belongs to the category of singers whose final acceptance came posthumously. Despite his sensational popularity, McCormack often felt the snub of the purist. . . .'; but surely he is mistaken in adding that: 'Today, the *cognoscenti* laud his art as they never did during his active career.' Critics who attended McCormack's recitals were not notably more restrained than the great mass of his audience. 'He has forgotten more than most singers know about phrasing, style, and the spirit of Mozart's music', wrote Olin Downes in the *New York Times*; Eugene Stinson of the *Chicago Daily News* described him as 'A beloved bard, a perfect instrumentalist of song. He is the ideal type of artist.' Rave reviews abound. Richard Capell in the London *Daily Mail* once wrote: 'Compared with John McCormack many professional singers are half amateur'; while W. J. Henderson of the New York *Sun*, whose memories went back further than most, declared: 'If there was ever a brilliant object lesson in any department of art, it has been furnished by John McCormack. . . . The musical style is the vocal revelation of the heart within the man.'

'He has become a national institution', wrote *The Pictorial Review* in 1916; and if a symbol of his being an American institution was required, it came with the Fourth of July celebrations of 1918, as recorded in *Musical America*, 11 July:

> . . . when he was invited by the committee in charge of the Fourth of July celebration in Washington to participate in the historic meeting held on the grassy Potomac slope where the Father of His Country is buried. The invitation was extended following a conference between George Creel, chairman of the committee and President Wilson.
>
> It was the one hundred and forty-second anniversary of the signing of the Declaration of Independence, and the meeting will

Famous Tenor Delighted with Experiences of Recent Southern Tour—Winter Plans Include Chicago Opera Appearances and Concerts in the West

CONVINCED that Southern hospitality is a delightful reality, John McCormack, the distinguished Irish tenor, has returned from a trip which took him to New Orleans, points, enthusiastic ov given to him by his aud one he met, socially an In many of the cities h formally received by me government and he ad had accepted all the luncheons and dinners he would not have bee note.

In every city visited local managers made one but two dates for n tour from beginning to plete triumph for Mr.

The first engagement ton, D. C., Nov. 26, w New National Theater Throughout the tour were decidedly in evide every place the entire sold out days before the n Dallas, Tex., that nthusiast who had bee daily papers for seat location desired and th price did not enter int

Visits One of Yo

Mr. McCormack had perience of singing in of the youngest cities being fifteen years old. was given under the Hyechka Woman's Club In Fort Worth, Tex., after the concert that turns had been so amp

McCORMACK FURORE
IN SAN FRANCISCO

Great Tenor Attracts Clamoring Throngs of Listeners —"Pop" Concert—Trio Heard—Auditorium Music

John McCormack achieved as great a success in San Francisco, judged by attendance and applause, as can be possible. The entire seating capacity of the great Exposition Auditorium was sold out in advance of the performance, and the day before the opening of the concert by McCormack it was impossible to buy a ticket for a seat, nc thousands of perman porarily placed chair from a score of cities cisco a chance to h the auditorium doors time in advance of sing, great crowds and would have paic than to have been sh accommodate them. was employed to sea were opened an hou concert to avoid a j

Notwithstanding t with a cold his voic wonderful enunciatio sympathy, caused th When the program. pleted, an audience the seats until the si "Drink to Me Only.

date in Dallas this season. He sang in Houston and in New Orleans. In the latter city the scale of prices charged for seats was on the Metropolitan Opera Company basis, ranging from $5 down with standing room at $3.

In January Mr. McCormack will sing in three performances with the Chicago Opera Co. in Chicago, the operas being "La Bohème" and "Don Giovanni." He will also give a concert in Chicago and will be heard later in January in Pittsburgh and Cincinnati. During February he will be in the West.

M'CORMACK SINGS
TO 4,000 AT CENTURY

Adds Comic "Kitty, Won't You Marry Me?" to His Ir
songs and Balla

Four thousand admirer McCormack filled the bi Theatre to overflowing day's first Winter storm. vance indications of a peared, the stage was hast of its mountains of Max I scenery. Even so, there eral hundred late-comer away from the matinée.

McCORMACK'S FIFTH GREATER NEW YORK RECITAL OF SEASON.

Huge Audience Seems Insatiate.

John McCormack gave his fifth Greater New York recital of the season, on Sunday afternoon, January 16, at Carnegie Hall. If one were to judge from the crow that frantically endeavored to get into the building, filling every box and seat in the house, overflowing on to the stage, and occupying every bit of standing room which the fire laws permitted, said judge would undoubtedly have concluded that the celebrated Irish tenor was about to retir and might never sing again in public; while on the contrary, he is announced for another appearance in the same hall on February 13.

As usual Mr. McCormack opened his program with a number which served to display the technical skill which underlies all of his work. Handel's "O Sleep, Why Dost Thou Leave Me?", with its many florid passages, was sung with rare beauty of tone and exceptional skill. "I Attempt from Love's Sickness to Fly," by Purcell, was also delightful, these two numbers serving to display Mr. McCormack's ability as a singer of classical music.

For his second group the tenor chose "In This Hour of Night" (Tschaikowsky), "The Gardener" (Hugo Wolf),

as that which filled the Athenæum to overflowing. Long before the date announced for the opening of the box office the house was practically sold out and at the last moment hundreds of music lovers purchased general admission tick ets and stood in the aisles of the upper galleries throughout the entire program.

Delight in Irish Folk Songs

Mr. McCormack was in splendid voice, and, living up to his reputation, was quite generous in encores. The program opened with two old classics of Handel, "Where'er You Walk"
.e," followed by song school, Bleichmann ell and Tschnikown h folk songs, "An I W gan Love Song," "Th and "The Cruiske ried the audience i ne and nothing less t

ORD RICHMOND AUDIENCE
GREETS McCORMACK.

rn Engagement of Irish Tenor—Over $5,000 Gross Receipts Taken In.

Richmond, Va., February 19, 1916.
t in the musical chronicles of this city has there been ded to a visiting artist on a return engagement than eption in point of numbers and enthusiasm as that ry 15 at the Auditorium, to the Irish tenor, nack. For the first time since it developed t house into a concert hall, so far as the mem un can recall, the City Auditorium's vast floor ony were not large enough to accommodate it clamored to buy seats, and chairs were sold the program with two superb Handel arias, he sang in magnificent style, displaying the uty of his voice and a breath control not ng. The program contained also a group of y Schubert, Schumann, Rachmaninoff and
His rendition of these completely capti ence, and he was forced to give several en ollicking "Nelly My Love, and Me," con up of Irish songs, but not according to the adience. The house took matters into its encore after encore was compelled and gen From the opening Handel numbers to the not only the pit, but the balcony, rose at he had finished the house actually rose and ling, applauding and even cheering until he sang again.
eider, the accompanist, provided such sup fr. McCormack and to Mr. McBeath as so e able to obtain.

would satisfy them. His last group menced with "When the Dew Is Fal by Edwin Schneider, Mr. McCorm able accompanist, who rose to receiv applause justly due him; "The Ol fmin," by Fritz Kreisler (a vic song, arranged and dedicated to Mr Cormack), and "If You Would Me," by James G. MacDermid, but continual applause brought Mr. Mc mack back for another encore. A close thousands left the auditorium luctantly and with the hope that great tenor would come back again

ST. PAUL BOX OFFICE RECORDS
BROKEN BY JOHN McCORMA

Irish Tenor Draws Usual Vast Throng of Admirers— Grainger Makes Initial Local Appearance and Scores Success.

St. Paul, Minn., February 9,
St. Paul's musical high lights of the past week

WESTERN UNION TELEGRAM

RECEIVED AT 1450 BROADWAY, NEW YORK
B165NYN 53

AX LOSANGELES CALIF NOV 21ST 1916 1155AM
CHARLES L WAGNER   884
1451 BROADWAY NY

THANKS FOR KIND TELEGRAM ABOUT FRISCO VOICE STILL LITTLE WEAK
STRONGLY ADVISE CUTTING DOWN TOUR TO FIFTY DATES THIS YEAR
YOU CAN ARRANGE I WILL SING EVERY SUNDAY AND ONE WEEK DAY
DOCTOR SAYS I SIMPLY MUST BE CAREFUL OR AN OTHER BOUT LIKE LAST
MAY KILL GOOSE THAT LAYS GOLDEN EGGS WARMEST GREETINGS
JOHN MCCORMACK
356P

ABOVE *A telegram from the tenor to h manager, dated 21 November 1916. T gruelling schedule of ninety-five concerts the 1914–15 season had taken its toll. Th seasons immediately following were hardl less strenuous; 1915–16: eighty-fiv concerts and two opera appearances 1916–17: about eighty concerts 1917–18: eighty-eight concerts and fiv opera appearances; 1918–19: about ninet concerts and two opera appearances. Th figure of fifty concerts did not ente McCormack's schedule (apart from sprin and autumn seasons) until the 1925–2 season.*

ALONGSIDE *Newsclips illustrate his success and his popularity.*

...down as one of the most important in the history of this country ...cause of the great speech ('a new Declaration of Independence') ...ivered by a great President, and because of the representative ...aracter of the gathering.

Thirty-three nationalities were represented. As each pilgrim ...ssed by President Wilson to lay a wreath on the tomb of ...ashington, as a token of fealty to the principles laid down by the ...ther of His Country, Mr McCormack, standing by his side, ...ng 'The Battle Hymn of the Republic'. Later on, following the ...esident's great speech, the singer mounted a slight eminence to ...e side of the tomb and sang 'The Star Spangled Banner'. ...oldiers, sailors and marines to the number of 1,000 stood at salute, ...d the thousands of citizens who were crowded on to the lawn ...ere thrilled by the noted tenor's spirited rendition of the national ...them.

Mr McCormack was a guest of the President on board the ...*Mayflower* on the trip from Washington to Mount Vernon and ...turn, and President Wilson extended his congratulations, ...armly grasping the singer by the hand and telling him it was the ...nest rendition of our anthem he had ever heard.

...honour was the more exceptional because McCormack was not, at ...ime, an American citizen. He did not become one until June 1919, ...years after he had made his first application in April 1914. No act ...to cause him more trouble. In accordance with the regulations ...erning applications for United States citizenship McCormack was ...uired, three years after his initial application, to declare his ...lingness to renounce all previous loyalties. On 27 January 1917, ...der the heading 'McCormack's Nationality', *The Times* announced ...ply that 'the Irish tenor has renounced his allegiance to King George ...d declared his intention of becoming a citizen of the United States', ...d made no further comment, but a section of the British public saw ...s move as an evasion of duty and obligation towards the war effort. ...e tenor became the recipient of abusive mail, and for a period his ...eer in England looked uncertain.

There were repercussions in Australia, too. As late as 1920 a concert ...r ran into trouble in Adelaide, as *The Times* reported, 11 September:

Owing to the omission of the National Anthem at Mr John McCormack's, the Irish tenor's concerts, a large crowd made a demonstration. Hundreds remained behind at the conclusion. Someone shouted 'Sinn Fein'. 'God save the King' was sung while the tenor was preparing to depart.

Irish First World War recruitment poster. The Austrian critic Eduard Hanslick once remarked that 'to win the favour of the British public is not easy; to lose it impossible.' McCormack lost it through his application for American citizenship. This was prompted mainly by the financial advantages it offered. He was not against the British cause as such, for he helped it in several ways: sending cigarettes to the troops, and supporting war charities. But the feeling at that time was that if you are not fighting for us, you must be against us. Ironically, it was to be in Britain during the Second World War that the tenor sang to his last and most loyal audiences.

"A Studied Insult"

Famous Tenor Arrives

"ATTEMPT TO EMBARRASS ME"

As Mr John M'Cormack, the famous tenor, stepped on to the Spencer street station from the Adelaide express this morning and joyfully acknowledged the salutations of a number of friends he did not look as if he had been the victim of "a studied insult" in the capital of South Australia. His face was wreathed in smiles and he grasped the hands of his friends affectionately.

"How are you, John?" asked Mr J. Tait, as he held out his hand, and the reply was that he was all right. The tenor was touched by the greetings, and temperament showed itself again when the abrupt closing of the Adelaide season was mentioned. Mr M'Cormack's face became overcast, and he emphatically declared that a studied insult was offered to him on Thursday evening by a small section of the audience at the Exhibition Building, Adelaide, and that he had suffered indignities elsewhere.

"The Obvious Insinuation"

"You do not know all," remarked Mr M'Cormack as the question was asked whether the singing of the National Anthem by a few people should have been sufficient to induce him to abandon his final concert in Adelaide.

"It was a studied insult," said Mr M'Cormack, "because of the obvious insinuation that I had refused either to sing the National Anthem or have it performed. Such an insinuation of a breach of common courtesy I consider a grave insult.

Newsclip from The Melbourne Herald, *September 1920. The incident in Adelaide forced McCormack to cancel not only his tour in Australia but his plans to appear in London on his return to Europe. He wrote to Charles L. Wagner on 2 October, expressing his feelings.*

Sydney
October 2nd, 1920

My Dear Charlie

Doubtless Mac has told you all the news of my final cancellation of the whole damn tour here so there is no further need for me to labour the question. I have only the most peculiar feelings in regard to this place. I have never seen such splendid loyalty and friendship on the one side and on the other the most outrageous rudeness and boorishness and discourtesy. Of course the people from whom I have recieved the latter treatment are now very anxious to make it appear that they did not mean to insult me for being an American but only for renouncing my allegiance to the emp This is rather cutting things rather fine. There is no doubt that t have never forgiven me for becoming an American and in fact one ma said in a public place that they would have forgiven me if I had b anything but a "damn Yank". We sail on the Naldmma next Wednesday D and should arrive in London about the 20th. November and will be at Carlton. I think however that all mail would be safer at the Americ Express as we may take a place as soon as we arrive there. I had a from Mary Scott last night and you will be sorry to hear that her brother Walter, I think you met him, died suddenly on the 14th. Augus' Quinlan writes most enthusiastically abut things in England and I f sure all will be well there. By the way I see it reported that the intend to have a season of Opera at Covent Garden next summer. Tell Gatti I would very much like to sing there with the Company and that the fee I will leave to himself. Of course the Covent Garden crowd d not want me there now but I would love to put one across them by appearing with the Metropolitan co. Some stunt boy put it over! When w arrive in London? Lily was told by a fortune teller the other day th I am to make a great success in Stockholm and such places in the Nox so I will expect to hear that you have fixed some dates there. Certai there will have to be some success at least socially there to make for the terrible time we have had here where we have been socially ostracised and avoided as one avoids lepers. I am glad however to hav suffered that for being an Irishman and an American. It is cheap at the price. I will have many stories for you when I see you.

We are all fine nevertheless and of course tickled to death to be getting out so soon. Greetings to everybody especially Bertha and Miss Holmes.

Best ever to your old self.

Yours as ever

John McCormack

Mr McCormack was visibly affected by this imputation of disloyalty, and has refused to appear in further concerts at Adelaide. It may involve the abandonment of the rest of his Australian tour. He is reported to be hurrying back to America.

The tour was cancelled.

Early in his career, songs of patriotism – of which Ireland has a long tradition – featured prominently in his repertoire of ballads. The early cylinders contain such examples as 'The Croppy Boy', 'A Nation Once Again', 'The Boys of Wexford' and 'The Wearing of the Green'. At the prizewinners' concert following the 1904 Feis Ceoil, the young tenor had suggested singing the militant 'The West's Awake', for which he had a reputation. In the event his other choice, 'The Snowy Breasted Pearl' was what he sang, and presumably it was what the committee in charge felt was appropriate. But when the other song was called for from the audience at a concert in England, he wisely refused to oblige. In *The Sword of Light*, Peter Dolan has suggested:

> McCormack seemed a naïve child in the face of conflicting nationalisms. Perhaps he had doubts about his own national identity. Both his parents were Scots [the nationality of the father has not in fact been definitely established], and he was born and brought up in Athlone, then a British garrison town. McCormack's parents had no roots in Athlone [this again is not certain] and his father was a foreman in the Athlone Woollen Mills, a largely Protestant industry.

It seems unlikely, however, that these elements influenced McCormack negatively, for the very reason that it was when they were at their strongest that he was singing nationalistic songs. Moreover, so unmistakably an Irish personality as McCormack possessed does not suggest doubts about national identity, though his relationship with Athlone always remained brittle. He may have had doubts about his *social* identity, but he always remained a nationalist in outlook.

But his conception of what he believed Irish nationalism ought to entail almost certainly underwent modification on his arrival in London. In this connection the most probable influence would have been Sir John Murray, to whose patronage the tenor owed so much; and it probably coincided with his entry into Sir John's house, the opulent and aristocratic life-style of which McCormack was so closely to imitate at Esher Place in Surrey, England, and at Moore Abbey in Ireland. It is significant that after his Covent Garden debut he recorded only one rebel song, and that was in America in 1912: 'The Wearing of the Green'.

When America entered the war in the spring of 1917, McCormack

McCormack singing at an open-air charity concert in America during the First World War.

contributed to the war effort by making a coast-to-coast concert tour on behalf of the Red Cross, at his own expense. By giving recitals, singing songs chosen by the public at high prices, and by auctioning autographed records, he raised an estimated half million dollars for the Liberty Bond Drive. He also sang for the Knights of Colombanus and other charities and his public appearances proved to be a potent force in keeping, as it was said, 'the home fires burning'.

McCormack had not sung in England since 1914 and he did not return until 1924. This was the year that Amelita Galli-Curci, whose legendary reputation had preceded her via her gramophone records, made her debut in England at the Albert Hall. The society press described it as the concert of the year. McCormack, playing safe, chose to appear in the smaller Queen's Hall. It was an unnecessary precaution, for he sang, as *The Times* put it: 'to an Albert Hall audience (or as many as could be packed in) in the Queen's Hall'. 'Of all the concerts I attended this was the most memorable', wrote Lily. Compton Mackenzie remembered it too:

'In two moods' – Bishop Curley
McCormack in Athlone. They ɾ
schoolboy friends, and when McCorɾ
was living in Noroton, Connectɪ
Curley was Bishop of the Diocese oɟ
Augustine, Florida. In 1918, Cha
Wagner arranged for a biography of
singer to be written: 'His own life stoɾ
transcribed by Pierre V. R. Key'. Cu
became a kind of literary adviser – a
Wagner did not approve of, because:
entire idea was altered. What was inteɾ
to be an authentic story turned out a ɩ
sentimental and unreal accouɪ
McCormack thought so too, and iɪ
perhaps the measure of the man that u
the book was published, he bought ouɪ
edition.

During that war he had spoken out strongly on behalf of his native country and in disgust at the English treatment of Ireland . . . now that peace had been made between Ireland and England, McCormack was anxious to sing again in London. . . . The announcement led to John's receiving a number of anonymous letters threatening what would happen to him if he dared show his face before a London audience. He did me the honour of inviting me to sit between the Countess and his daughter in case there was an unpleasant demonstration. I had just grown a black beard about that time and looked a bit fierce. John himself spent the whole day in church after communicating at early mass, and from the church he came straight to Queen's Hall. The place was packed. I sat between the tenor's wife and daughter in the middle of the front row of the circle. I can see now John's face, chalk white as he came on to the platform. There was a moment's silence and then the audience broke into mighty applause and cheering. John's face grew whiter, if possible. A silence fell. Then as if from another world he started the aria 'O Sleep' on that high opening note without the ghost of a tremolo in it. The return to London was a triumph, and not one of the gallant band of anonymous letterwriters ventured as loud a hiss as a moulting gander. We had a wonderful supper party that night and a few days later John played over to me the records he had just made of Brahms and Wolf.

Brahms and Wolf – and 1924. The date is of interest because it was the year which Grove's *Dictionary of Music and Musicians* (in the fifth edition, which was published after the tenor's death) chose to divide McCormack's career into two. The Dictionary claimed:

> [By 1924] he could no longer be taken altogether seriously as a musician, since in his later years he devoted his extraordinary and unimpaired gifts to largely sentimental and popular ditties, not to be listened to with patience by critics or with enjoyment by true music lovers.

And so the legend remains: a singer of popular ballads and tunes who prostituted his greater accomplishments for wider and commercial application of lesser, sometimes worthless material. Grove's Dictionary was not, of course, alone in making such a criticism. It was a common cry of many music critics. O. L. Whalen in *The Detroit Journal*, for example, went so far as to say:

> John McCormack, being from Athlone in the very heart of Ireland, and knowing the entrancing folk art of his land, could stand with Yeats and Lady Gregory as an exponent of it, and the encouragement which his audiences give should make it wonderfully agreeable, yet he chooses to sing dozens of foolish ditties and places himself only a little higher than Mary Pickford and Harold Bell Wright, who exploit the art of no country but merely purvey cheap sentimentality.

But Grove's Dictionary was unique in providing a specific date in its assessment. The year 1924 happens to have been the year Compton Mackenzie met the tenor for the first time, when the author was a 'guest of the Irish Nation' at the Tailteann Games in Dublin. It was a revealing meeting:

> One of the keenest pleasures in an artist's life is to be able to tell another artist quite sincerely that he admires his work. 'Yes, but I expect you think I sing a great deal of rubbish', said McCormack to me. I agreed and suggested that for this side of the Atlantic he had sung enough. 'Yes, but I'm going to sing Wolf and Brahms now, and all sorts of songs that I really want to sing.' 'That's the best news I've heard for a long time,' I assured him.

In the previous year the tenor had made a tour of Middle Europe and emphasized his Lieder repertoire – this may account for the date Grove chose. In 1924 he recorded seven compositions by Schubert, Brahms

In the spring of 1922, McCo developed a near-fatal streptococcal infection. Wagner wrote to him in En where he was recuperating, to suggest a series of concerts in the States later year. McCormack's reply is of s interest as it contains some of his fe and ideas about his career.

June 24th '12

Dear Charles,

Your favor of John mine here. Please do believe me at last once. I am not going back this year to work in America whether I have a hunch or not. Let me show you a few reasons. If I go back for say twenty concerts I will have the enormous expense of ocean travel coming to something like £100. I will get in money from Ed something like £60,000 that added to my Victor check brings in Income Tax up by £25,000, so that in the last analysis I will be getting £500 for 20 concerts and out of it pay enormous hotel expenses and stop my treatment in New York. Charles I won't do it. Secondly I have had a very severe illness and feel I need to rest until such time as I can safely do a tour without the danger of a

reputation, and I am going to work for it. I have made arrangements to study German lieder with Dr. Lange Muncheid this fall and Teddy and I are then going in the spring to sing in Berlin and other large German cities and Vienna and I am going to find out once for all whether I am just a ballad singer or a real singer. If you were an artist you would know that to sing always for the same public is very tiresome for the singer and makes him or he inclined to be lackadaisical and slipshod in method. I want to jack myself up as it were so that I can if possible sing more to my American public that I dearly love, and I want my American public to be proud of their American singer, and to share in any success that may be mine over here. I refuse to believe that with the American public it is a case of "out of sight, out of mind." I protest against the libel on the most generous public in the world. I have spoken to many Americans of my decision to take the year off and they have all

nervous breakdown as well as a physical one. I have worked very hard in America for many years and have had very little recreation. I feel that while I am young I should have the fun out of life and not wait till I am an old man. Caruso worked himself to death and what did he get out of life? As to the fickleness of the American public I disagree entirely from you. I believe that the American public likes and admires and may to lean the artist that can enhance the goods and so only fickle to you believe the goods and not the artist does not like that word why the artist does not deserve the good. Believe me if I were to return to America and on account of a slight cold had to cancel some concerts or sang badly for any reason or had another experience like Minneapolis then I believe the American public would become fickle and would then believe that my voice was seriously injured by my very serious illness I feel strongly there is more in life than money besides. I want a world wide

without a single exception said God knows you need a rest after your hard work and that heavy illness in the spring. Therefore Charles if you are writing to me again Don't try to make me change my mind for I won't do it. I am enclosing you a copy of Sir Bruce Bruce Porter's letter to Teddy which you will note is endorsed by Sir St Clair Thomson and that letter covers the whole thing. I am not trying to loaf but I am determined not to let anyone sing me to death. I am determined to live my life and have a jolly good time out of it. Surely you won't begrudge me a holiday and a rest. Greetings to you both hope to see you in July and I will surely have you both meet Mary Anderson.

Yours as ever
John McCormack.

and Wolf, the largest number he was to record in any one year; but he continued to sing German Leider for the rest of his career.

The assumption that McCormack's choice of concert material deteriorated with the years does not stand up to examination. It was as a ballad singer that McCormack began. In his first concerts in 1903 and 1904, when he might be said to have some pretensions towards being a professional singer, he concentrated mainly though not exclusively on Irish ballads. Three years later he sang in his first opera and, following a stint in London concert halls in 1907 prior to his Covent Garden debut, he could never again be described as 'nothing other than a singer of ballads'. On 18 October 1910 he gave one of his first major London recitals, at Queen's Hall, with Mario Sammarco. We find that the first half of the programme was given up to opera; McCormack sang 'Che Gelida Manina' from *La Bohème*, Sammarco sang 'Largo al Factotum' from *The Barber of Seville*. Only in the second half did the tenor introduce his Irish ballads, and then the concert was wound up with the Quartet from *Rigoletto* with the assisting artists.

During his first years in America, McCormack followed a similar pattern. Then, around 1913, he began to include less nineteenth-century opera and to turn increasingly to eighteenth-century classical arias and Lieder. In the 1915–16 season in New York, in twelve concerts, he did not repeat one song or aria in twelve different programmes, excluding encores. In December 1924 he outlined how he planned his concerts in *Musical America*:

> The first group of songs which I give, on any programme, are songs which I sing to please myself. They represent my musical taste. The second group is made up of art songs, that is to say, fine songs which the public should like and which it will like once they are heard a sufficient number of times to become familiar.
>
> The third group I give contains the beautiful Irish folk-songs which have survived the ages because of the deathless appeal they make to the hearts of men. . . . The fourth group of songs represents the fine work of modern American and English composers. . . .

On his return to London in the same year, *The Times* of 6 October congratulated him on:

> A very substantial programme. He did not propose the three hackneyed arias with a few ballads, which famous singers often think, no doubt correctly, are good enough for such an audience, but gave a scheme of songs in four groups, calculated to show very different sides of his art which, in the years since he was heard here, he has developed considerably.

tenor with Sir Edward Elgar
57–1934) in 1932. A full-length
rding of The Dream of Gerontius,
McCormack singing the title part and
composer conducting was mooted, but
e to nothing.

Nor do we find any falling off later in his career. Moving on ten years to the Albert Hall on 1 December 1934 we find: 'His programme contained something of almost everything, though modern opera was unrepresented in the scheme'. The scheme consisted of 'setting Brahms by the seventeenth century Dr Howard and Handel between Parry and Schumann. . . .' Two years later: 'Handel's name occurred most frequently, and it suits Mr McCormack well, but he also put in an example of Wolf, of Parry ('Armida's Garden') and of Franck ('Panis Angelicus').' Even as late as 1941, three years after his official retirement when there was not a great deal of voice left, in a concert given in the small English town of Watford, for example, he sang Handel and Rachmaninov. And in the States, the composition of his programmes had been similar. So however much Grove's Dictionary and company might disapprove of the inclusion of popular songs and ballads in the tenor's programmes, the fact remains that even by their own standards there was material in plenty by which the tenor might be judged a musician or no.

The discography is, however, another matter. Out of six hundred-odd recorded sides, less than a handful are from the tenor's 'first group' of songs. Handel is represented by five items. But of these only two – 'Come my beloved' (1924) and 'O, Sleep why dost thou leave me?' (1920) – were recorded in the singer's prime. Of the other three, 'Praise Ye the

Lord' from *Cantata con Strumenti* was recorded in 1941, and 'Where e'er You Walk' and 'Caro Amor' were both recorded in 1936. There are five Mozart compositions, but of these, two – 'Ave Verum' and 'To Chloe' – belong to McCormack's very last recording session, which took place on 10 September 1942, and can hardly be regarded as representative of his art. 'Oh, What Bitter Grief is Mine' was recorded only two years earlier, in December 1940. 'Ridente la Calma' was recorded in 1924 and demonstrates the marvellous symmetry of phrase that McCormack possessed, though the top is by no means as fresh as it would have been three or four years earlier. Only 'Il Mio Tesoro' (1916) belongs to the tenor's absolute vocal prime. Arguably the most important Mozartian and Handelian tenor in the century, this is a chronically poor leavening for posterity. A glance at almost any ten or twelve of McCormack's programmes show what eighteenth-century music he maintained in his repertoire and might have recorded. His work in oratorio is represented by the recitative and aria from Beethoven's *Christ on the Mount of Olives*, and it demonstrates the tenor's marvellous feeling for that idiom. There is, however, no other oratorio material on record, unless one includes the 'Champs Paternels' from Méhul's Biblical opera *Joseph*.

There is no doubt that the lighter material predominates at the expense of much that we would like to hear. Some of the ditties seem a bit thin now. But brave the man who would say that McCormack should not have recorded x or y. It is sure to be someone's favourite. One does not, in any case, have to listen to any particular item. One cannot, however, listen to what was never recorded. The abnegation of responsibility lay not, as some would have it, in what McCormack recorded, but in what he omitted. His discography served contemporary needs better than it now serves posterity.

There is, perhaps, a parallel to be drawn between McCormack and the French soprano Emma Calvé. So popular an impression did Calvé make in the title role of Carmen that her other, and in her own opinion greater, achievements were overlooked. So it was to a substantial extent with McCormack. His repertoire was vastly greater in so-called 'art songs' than ever his public knew. He was one of the two best sight-readers in Gerald Moore's experience, Fischer-Dieskau being the other; and Lily in *I Hear You Calling Me* recalled an evening when: 'John sang straight through two volumes of Hugo Wolf's songs, with Rachmaninov at the piano and Ernest Newman turning the pages.'

He was an inveterate collector of music, hunting through antiquarian bookshops and browsing in any likely spot where he might turn up something unusual. To sing these finds for hours of a morning with Teddy Schneider was for McCormack a vocal way of life, and what the gramophone may have lost from such pickings we shall never know. In so far as any singer may be said to have achieved it, McCormack was, in concert, all things to all men. Most men wanted to hear him in ballads and songs, and it is thus as a singer of ballads and songs that most men remember him. It is now a commonplace to say that McCormack sang his ballads without a trace of condescension. Moreover, he was, as Ernest Newman put it, 'so perfect in small things because he was steeped in greater ones'. It is demonstrable: one can point to the same immaculate vocal line in each, to the same lucid diction, the identical craftsmanship. So much is a matter of common agreement.

But what about the converse? Can McCormack's achievements in the classics of song be said to have derived anything from his immersion in popular songs? I believe it can, and the question is of particular importance because of the tenor's position in vocal history. There was a saying that McCormack made it when everyone had a gramophone and no one a radio; but he made it on radio too. It might be more relevant to the question to say that McCormack made it when everyone had a radio but no singer a microphone.

red, from the left, are Dennis F. ...weeney, John McCormack and ...y Schneider. McSweeney, a Kerry ...met McCormack when the tenor was ...g at the Manhattan in 1909. 'At ... according to Wagner, 'his wild ...ation was so extreme it annoyed the ...Cormacks. Later, when I had him ...ss it to press material on our tenor, it ...effective and contributive. He could ...ce no such copy for any other artist, ...or John it was telling and convincing.' ...weeney worked for McCormack, ...during his period with the Wolfsohn ...au; and then joined Wagner as ...iate manager – usually taking care of ...ls 'on the road'. In 1924 McCormack ...McSweeney sole charge of his affairs.

4 A PERSPECTIVE

Al Jolson, at the end of a live radio broadcast in the United States in 1932, took hold of the microphone, threw it to the floor, and exclaimed to the audience in the studio: 'It's a sad day when Jolie needs a mike to sing into.' He then proceeded to give a demonstration of his vocal powers without it. Today, his gesture seems curiously anachronistic; and so it was, even as he made it; for the inseparable association of the microphone with the popular vocalist had already begun to manifest itself in the second half of the twenties.

Traditionally, the opera singer has eschewed the microphone, seeing in its employment a threat to the integrity of his vocal production. Whereas, in theory, it might be used solely to supply additional volume and ease some of the demands made on the singer's vocal stamina, consistent use would almost certainly lead in practice to the development of new and, to the opera singer, alien vocal sounds. The popular singer, on the other hand, having had no vocal tradition as comparably defined – or circumscribed – to safeguard against change, felt free to exploit the new sounds opened up by the microphone. And whether the popular singer is conscious of the fact or not, he has gone even further than that, for in a sense the microphone has made it possible to set the laws of acoustic physics on their head. By judicious use of the instrument, virtually any sound, whatever its level of sonority or carrying power, can be given *any degree of prominence* that the singer desires. Thus, irrespective of how small or intimate his audience may be, the singer for whom the microphone is truly an inherent part of his art cannot sing in the same way without it. Nor will he sound the same without it, however much or little volume he himself produces. The prime value of the microphone lies not simply in the fact that it augments volume *per se*, but because it offers dynamic perspectives not otherwise available. Thus it is possible to

speak of the microphone singer and of the 'serious' or opera singer not as one being a vocal miniature of the other, but rather as two distinct generic categories of singing, arising from the different use of the vocal mechanism both physiologically and stylistically.

It is a truism to say that compositions derive structural characteristics from the instrument for which they are written. The microphone cannot be described as a musical instrument on its own, but the voice amplified by a microphone is an entirely different instrument from the one associated with European vocal music. The difference is one of vocal idiom. The opera singer exploits melodic flight, vocal soaring, thrilling altitudes, a fine legato line, an extensive vocal range. The verbal aspect of a song or aria, German Lieder and early *recitative* opera excepted, is of secondary importance, even incidental. At best the melodic and verbal

The only known photograph of the e McCormack family, taken in the gard the house the tenor bought for his fe Back row, from left: Lily, John, Mar Aggie (sisters), James (brother). Se Hannah and Andrew. Front row: G doline, Cyril (the children); and Fl another sister.

lines move in parallel. By comparison, for the 'popular' singer it is the natural rhythms of speech, its inflexions and cadences, that comprise the very source of his melodic utterance. Composers and arrangers of serious and popular vocal music are writing, therefore, for two different voices, and neither voice is well adapted to the music belonging to the other.

'Popular' (pop) music means American music (Afro-American if you prefer) or some European derivation of it. This music pre-dates the microphone as does the vocalist we now describe as 'popular', but by the time the serious or opera singer might have wished to sing it – when its popularity was becoming widespread and eating into the popularity of European music – the microphone had arrived. The serious singer had, therefore, to compete with the popular microphone singer; and this he was ill-equipped to do, not because he could not sing the music, but because he could not sing it idiomatically. He took Afro-American music in the same way as European music, as instrumentally oriented as opposed to what it was and is: verbally oriented music. And the microphone magnified the idiomatic difference by bringing the verbal aspect of Afro-American music on to an altogether more intimate plane.

When John McCormack began his career in opera, this dichotomy between voices had hardly been mooted. Singers and singing comprised, for the most part, a homogeneous hierarchy, with the most beautiful voices, the most skilful singers, occupying the most prestigious institution – the opera – and receiving comparable rewards. But all singers, wherever placed on the social and aesthetic scale, produced fundamentally the same kind of sound, and they sang fundamentally the same kind of music. There was only one kind of vocal hierarchy and it was possible to move up it or down it. And some did, like Lina Cavalieri, whose career as a café 'chanteuse' preceded her debut at Covent Garden; or the unfortunate, thriftless Tetrazzini, whose singing days ended in vaudeville.

Just how homogeneous was that hierarchy before the rise of the microphone voice is illustrated by a story the variety artist Gracie Fields relates in her autobiography, *Sing As We Go*. Tetrazzini paid a visit during the days of her operatic fame to the Lyceum Theatre, London. Gracie was appearing in *The Show's the Thing*.

> 'What's she doing here?' I panted as I came off, but the answer was waiting for me. Apparently she had heard that although I came on stage as a scrub-woman and clowned my way through half a dozen operatic arias in a mixture of Lancashire, Italian and French, I was getting all the top notes. Now she had sent a note round asking if I would sing the aria from *La Traviata* for her.

There was only one thing to do, go on stage and guy the aria she had requested, as I usually did. [The straight singing of operatic arias was by no means an uncommon feature of music hall.] I went, but I was quaking.

. . . when I got to my dressing-room the great singer was there waiting for me . . . her dark eyes were filled with tears. She was a little woman, and she stood on tip-toe and put up both her arms to embrace me. I wanted to cry too. I hugged her back, clumsily.

'My dear,' she said, 'oh, my dear, you *must* sing in opera. . . .'

The opera was then an institution which had claims to be generally intelligible, and generally popular. Its pre-eminence was unquestioned and unchallenged, but even as the Edwardians were relishing the delights of the great vocal personalities of the age: Melba, Tetrazzini, Kurz, Caruso, Chaliapin and so on, the last operatic works of widespread appeal had been written. Nothing subsequent to *La Bohème*, *Cavalleria Rusticana*, *Madama Butterfly* or *Tosca* has found as wide an audience, and of these operas only *Madama Butterfly* and *Tosca* received their first performance in this century. And only one operatic aria, 'Vesti la Giubba' from *I Pagliacci*, has found its way into Joseph Murrells' *Book of Golden Discs* which claims to list all million-selling records. Only one other singer of the operatic genre, Alma Gluck, is represented in the same catalogue, and not with an operatic aria but with 'Carry Me Back to Old Virginny', an American ballad.

For opera, as for so much else, the First World War is said to have marked the end of an era. What in fact had ended? Standards? Perhaps, but on that there is no general agreement. But it is certain that the opera had become less fashionable. The institution was losing credibility; and this loss coincided with McCormack's rising popularity as a recitalist. 'I always thought,' wrote the American critic Max de Schauensee, 'that McCormack was to the concert platform what Caruso was to opera.' The comparison holds good in so far as McCormack and Caruso were, during their lifetimes, without a rival in their respective fields. But whereas Caruso is regarded as a thrilling climax to a tradition of operatic tenors that stretched back at least one hundred and fifty years, McCormack could not be regarded as a climax to a tradition of recitalists. The recital had had no comparable history.

Offered less substantial rewards, the recitalist in the past tended to be vocally less well-endowed than his operatic counterpart. The recital, the soirée, the musical salon of the nineteenth century, so essential for the nurturing of young voices and probably for the maintenance of vocal traditions, was, nevertheless, an adjunct to the opera, an arena for those

A matching pair of tenors. While d with McCormack in the Savoy taurant, London, Caruso did a p sketch of the Irish tenor and of himse the back of two restaurant cards. McCormack sketch bears the inscript

RESTAURANT.

*my dearest friend MacCormack,
:o Caruso.' The sketches are not
, but if the Italian's receding hair is
ing to go by, then they were done
g his – and McCormack's – last
ent Garden season : 1914.*

whose disposition or ability did not equip them for the stage, and for the stars of the opera when they appeared off stage. Not surprisingly, the recital programme tended to depend heavily on operatic fare.

McCormack's art, hardly less than for the great operatic singers, derived from his training in and for opera, but no reputation among the great singers had ever depended less upon an operatic career. It is true that Jenny Lind, whose career in the States is sometimes compared with McCormack's, took American city after city by storm, giving only recitals in 1850–51, more than half a century before the tenor. But Lind certainly did not make the recital an independent institution. Her retirement from the opera was more apparent than real, for her concert repertoire, such as it was, depended heavily upon her operatic one. Nor did the furore she caused last long. At the end of a year, when she severed her connection with the impresario who had brought her to the States, Phineas Barnum, 'the mainspring of the whole undertaking', as her biographer Joan Bulman has put it, 'seemed to have given way.'

By any standards, staying power was a notable feature of McCormack's career. On 27 March 1932, twenty-three years after his first concert appearance in the States, he gave his one hundred and eightieth concert in New York city. This one took place at Carnegie Hall and was given to a capacity audience which included stage and standing room. It was subsequently described on a programme, probably quite accurately, as constituting 'a record unparalleled in the history of concertizing throughout the world'. His career was centred in, but not confined to, the States. His concert tours stretched from North America and Europe to Australia and New Zealand, South Africa, China and Japan; and but for the fact that Covent Garden refused to release him from his contract, he would probably have sung in Russia and South America as well.

With Caruso's passing in 1921, McCormack's celebrity in the States was without a rival. In the twenties he continued to combine, albeit uneasily, the dual role of 'serious' and 'popular' artist. The hazards were increasing. American popular music was finding an expanding audience and the divide between so-called serious and popular singers was becoming more apparent. The difficulties might have been greater for McCormack had not the twenties been the era of the 'big band'. American popular vocalists were not yet the big personalities they were to become. They often posed as instrumentalists in the big bands and strummed rubber-stringed guitars. Their names were not regarded as sufficiently prestigious to warrant appearance on the bands' record labels.

The gramophone had, by now, achieved an independent status of its

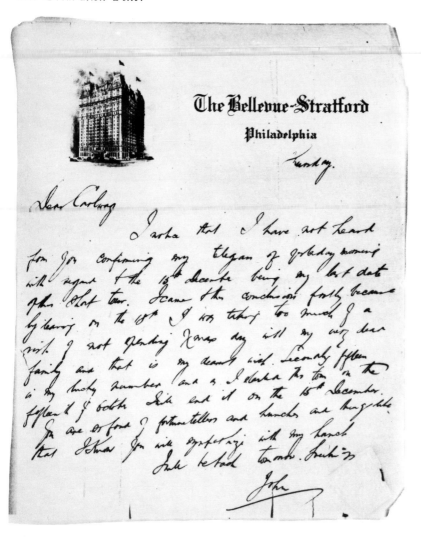

The Bellevue-Stratford
Philadelphia

[handwritten letter]

own. McCormack made use of that independence by recording material which he probably would not have dared, and perhaps would not have cared, to include in his recital programmes. The *Gramophone* magazine, established in England in 1923, dealt mainly with 'serious' music and record reviews but retained a section for material not to be so regarded, entitled: 'Miscellaneous Records'. McCormack appeared in this section, for the first time, in May 1926. The reviewer exclaimed:

> I've caught a big fish in my net this month – no less than John McCormack . . . one of those indiscretions which are commonplaces of the Victor Bulletins but seldom survive the Atlantic passage. To be sure there was Mario Chamlee singing

'Me Neenyah' not long ago on Brunswick; so why not McCormack in 'Oh, How I Miss You Tonight' and 'You Forgot to Remember' (Irving Berlin)?

For a body of the tenor's admirers, the reviewer answered his own question in his following statement: 'The latter is sung by another celebrity, Al Jolson, on Brunswick.' There were other records by McCormack with similar associations; most notably Al Jolson's own composition, 'Sonny Boy', the first disc from the talkie era to sell a million copies. McCormack recorded it in 1928, the same year as Jolson. 'Three O'Clock in the Morning' was another major hit of the twenties. The recording by Paul Whiteman and his band sold an estimated three and a half million copies. McCormack anticipated Whiteman by a year, recording it in 1922, complete with the middle section of echoes of Big Ben, an exotic touch for a piece published in New Orleans.

For the 'serious' music critic, McCormack singing Victorian ballads and material familiar to soirées and even music halls was one thing; Afro-American popular music was another. At least one Victorian ballad, 'Home, Sweet Home', was absolutely indispensable to any self-respecting soprano. Tetrazzini omitted it from her first concert in London and was chided by *The Graphic* of 14 December 1907: 'If she imagines she can retain her hold upon the affection of the British public without it, it is to be feared that she is doomed to disappointment . . . [her] daring will lead to disastrous results.' The dubious musical value of such songs seems to have been of no consequence, and likewise Neapolitan folk-songs, the staple diet of Caruso and all Italians off stage. Because of their virile and operatic character and because they are heard in a foreign language critics happily overlooked the fact that 'Funiculì, Funiculà' or 'Maria, Maria', for example, are hardly substantial music.

The point is that, however reservedly McCormack's embracing of Victorian ballads and the like might have been viewed in serious musical quarters, it was nevertheless accepted that such music could be subject to elevation, unpropitious though such elevation might be. A similar tolerance was unlikely to be accorded to American music. This was not primarily, I believe, because the new idiom could not be accommodated in European vocal traditions (it is a lot more melodious and singable than much modern serious music) but because American music, especially after the inception of the microphone, was inevitably associated with a different way of singing, a different vocal aesthetic, and a different manipulation of vocal sounds. This aesthetic was rightly seen as a threat to the homogeneity and pre-eminent position of the vocal aesthetic of the serious singer. For McCormack to sing American popular music was not just a matter of crossing a qualitative boundary: it was a cultural one. Conversely, there were limits to the receptivity an audience oriented towards Afro-American music would have for a singer whose vocal identity was essentially alien to it. As this music and the microphone singer became increasingly a major reflection of contemporary taste, so European music and the 'serious' vocalist became increasingly a minor one, even to the point when, as J. B. Steane has put it in *The Grand Tradition*:

> To the average youngster, the sound of the operatic soprano voice on records is quite actively unpleasant, it sounds unnatural. . . . The male operatic voice is easier to take, and most will see, in a theoretical kind of way, that there is something in it. But singing means something else . . . its purpose is to express a lifestyle which is in utter opposition to all that grand opera and its traditions seem to them to stand for.

Closer to the old lifestyle than the new, McCormack was a representative of neither; and it was between the decline of the opera and the rise of the microphone that he was the manifestation of an age.

More than with any other music in his repertoire, audiences found an affinity with McCormack's renditions of rural Irish and Irish-style ballads. The same affinity could not exist today. Western society is now too urban-minded, and the Ireland into which McCormack was born has been transformed. The Irish famines of 1845 and 1846 forced an immediate mass exodus of a million people from the land, and endorsed a tradition of emigration that continued on for more than a century. Between 1881 and 1926 almost a million and a half left Ireland for the major cities of England, America and elsewhere. The emigrant communities formed a substantial part of the tenor's audiences, vociferously responding to his encores after, it was said, 'sitting through the classics in impatient silence'.

In Ireland today more than one in four still works on the land, and the countryside remains still unspoilt, but the relationship between the people and the rural land has undergone change. Economic expectations are now centred in the towns and in industrial development. At the turn of the century no such expectations existed. Ireland then consisted mainly of poor and often wretchedly squalid rural and village communities. Life was a struggle; tears were at the heart of things and were implicit in the tenor's voice. His art was a sublimation of that rural way of life. It was a way of life which passed with the arrival of 'the new Ireland', as it is often called, and the dramatic economic expansion of the late 1950s and 1960s. With it came a new urban man

...*Cormack and his accompanist, Edwin ...eider, at Muckross Abbey, Co. ...y, 1924. Schneider, ten years older ...McCormack, quiet and self-effacing ...ture, proved to be an ideal complement ...e extrovert and highly-strung tenor. ...ner brought them together in 1912. ...eider then replaced Spencer Clay and ...ined as McCormack's accompanist ...1937, when the singer retired from the ...rican concert circuit. According to ...gner, when he took over as ...Cormack's manager: 'Some com- ...ities hesitated to engage him ...Cormack] because they felt he could ...resent programs of sufficient quality or ...entic musicianship. I was determined to ...ect that. . . . Schneider was enthusiastic ...t this development towards classical ...tery of the literature of song. . . . He ...ained with John throughout his entire ...er, and most of the time, I fear, was a ...er poorly paid accompanist considering ...worth of his contribution and his ...acity for work. Singers are seldom ...rous to assistant artists.'*

with an aspiration towards a cosmopolitan identity and a reaction against the brogue and ballad of old. Irish rural ballads can never again have a contemporary significance. And the fact that McCormack's status as an artist is widely underrated in Ireland today has, I suspect, much to do with his rural associations. For a later generation, which is assured of its urban identity, McCormack's renderings of Irish ballads may take on the aura of a classical and rural remoteness.

Like many another celebrity, McCormack the man generated a certain amount of controversy. No one could question the richness of his personality or the wealth of boyish charm. And for a circle of intimates the man was loved no less than his art. Others who knew him less well were not always sure where they stood with him. The change from village lad to international celebrity could not have been easy. He relished his fame but was uncertain about his status. He resented and probably felt ill at ease with those who treated him with awe, while those who overstepped the bounds of familiarity could find themselves the recipients of a wit none too tactful, and that the tenor was capable, as Ernest Newton put it, of 'language so earthy that a docker might have blushed to hear him'.

'Strange that the first "words" we had in our married life', wrote Lily in *I Hear You Calling Me*, 'were because of John's extravagance.' Newly acquired wealth often gives rise to extremes. Francesco Tamagno – the

LEFT *McCormack at the Cu Racecourse, Co. Kildare. McCor had a long-held ambition to win the E Derby. It remained expensively unful*

Wagner noted that the tenor's managers in America emphasized nationality and regarded that as unnecessary tactic. John McCor never belonged solely to the Irish rac belonged to the entire musical w Nevertheless, McCormack, showman he was, knew perfectly well the value Irish image, and he made sure that it kept well to the fore. This was how a York Herald interview was report October 1928: 'There's more mone horseflesh, my boy, than there is in sin Remember that. While I was in Irela read that a racehorse had been sold seventy thousand pounds. Think o' Seventy thousand. And what d suppose I get as a tenor? Oh, no – Th not a doubt about it. Horse-breeding's business.

But I guess you've heard enough a that. Well . . . I wonder who won the today over in England? D'ye think ye phone me when ye find out? Thanks, boy. God bless ye, me lad. Now, th sweet of ye.'

enchant for champions: Lily ...rmack, Cecily Nelson (friend of ...amily), Maurice McLoughlin ...bledon champion), Gwen ...rmack, Michael Beary (Aga Khan ..., Edgar Wallace, Elsworth Vines ...bledon champion), and the tenor, ...t his house San Patrizio, Holly- ...in 1932. This, incidentally, was the ...otograph ever taken of Wallace.

A galaxy of stars of the twenties, photographed in New York during a party held in the house of the musician Ernest H. Schelling (1876–1939). 'Me', seated in the middle, is McCormack. Also in the photograph are the conductors Leopold Stokowski, Artur Bodansky and Frank Damrosch; the violinists Josef Hollman and Efrem Zimbalist; the painists Alexander Lambert and Artur Schnabel, and singers Marcella Sembrich, Alma Gluck and Maria Jeritza.

The tenor in September 1936, photo with Colonel Fritz Brasé, conducto Free State Army School of Music.

son of a small-time restaurateur in Piedmont – would surreptitiously fold his chicken bones and leftovers into his napkin, ostensibly 'for the dog', but in reality for himself. McCormack would have had little affinity for such antics. He amassed, among much else, a first-rate art collection and a string of, to his chagrin, less than first-rate racehorses. Upon a constitution not naturally disposed towards counting the cost, Lily exercised a restraining and perhaps crucial influence.

Even as performers go, McCormack was extremely highly-strung. He found release from the strain of continual touring in high living. It did not combine well with a tendency towards obesity. At an early age he presented a rotund figure and one who was in less than a state of prime physical fitness. One wonders what effect that may have had on the voice.

Though McCormack's vocal range contracted early – A and below became the congenial territory after 1922, when he was afflicted by a streptococcal throat infection – his voice nevertheless remained throughout the twenties a finely honed instrument; and in the first half of that decade, not far short of its original prime. And his records in the twenties continued to reveal his extraordinary span of repertoire and an idiomatic security, seemingly unaffected by how the material was juxtaposed in the studio. On 1 April 1920, for example, he recorded with 'The Barefoot Trail' and 'Wonderful World of Romance' the aria 'O, Sleep Why Dost Thou Leave Me?' from Handel's *Semele*. Fortunate was the generation who heard it in person. So finely sculpted are the phrases, so easeful the vocal line, that the text is evoked by the vocal production alone. Despite the long arduous phrases in this aria, it was wholly typical of McCormack to be able to make the attack on each ensuing phrase without any intimation of plosiveness, so often the ungainly concomitant to a long-drawn line. In concert, the purity of tone must have been a revelation in so taxing an aria. More is the pity, therefore, that this recording sounds so far back. The decade just ended was notorious for studio technicians playing safe.

Also in 1920, McCormack recorded two songs by Sergei Rachmaninov, the first of several. 'O Cease Thy Singing, Maiden Fair', originally set to a poem by Pushkin, McCormack sang in a translation he had made himself in collaboration with Teddy Schneider. How well he declaims the opening title-line, using the freedom of recitative to weight the phrase in favour of its verbal meaning. The firmness of the line throughout the song is never at fault, and the difficult key changes are made without ambiguity. The uniformity of vocal tone and colour, the freedom from aspirates and the firmness of line exhibited in this song or in 'When Night Descends' (which follows it on record RCA RB 6525) or indeed the *berceuse* from *Jocelyn* which preceded it, have perhaps no equal. Few singers have approached McCormack's facility for being able to take his legato line for granted. And I suspect it was this facility which enabled him to use consonants, especially at the beginning of words, to such great effect. It was largely his ability to apply various weights to leading consonants that enabled him to throw, at will, any word or group of words into relief without at the same time disturbing the essential smoothness of his legato line. It is difficult to think of another singer whose vocal modulations were made more for musical and verbal purposes and less from physical necessity.

All the more extraordinary, therefore, that so immaculate a craftsman could never sound precious. In the Rachmaninov songs the technical difficulties appear superfluous. Less fatalistic than a Russian might be inclined to make it – less overbearing, certainly, than the Hungarian Boris Christoff has made it – McCormack's recording of 'O, Cease Thy Singing, Maiden Fair' is pervaded by a ceaseless yearning, the song's essence. If there is a fault to be found in this record, it is perhaps only in the extreme broadness of the 'A' vowel, as in 'land'. Yearning turns to tranquillity in 'Come My Beloved' from Handel's *Atalanta*, recorded in 1924. This recording is well forward, and as clearly as anything McCormack put on record it reveals his well-nigh flawless ability to float the voice as if on the tip of the breath. The most notable feature of the record is his pianissimo high A that is sung to the word 'arms' in the phrase 'guide me gently to her arms'. The vowel is quietly but deftly attacked, the singer drops a tone, rises again with perfect security, rolls the 'r', murmurs the 'm', intimates the sibilant, all on a mere thread of sound, all clearly articulated. The sheer virtuosity of this feat probably obscures an even greater virtue. Despite the division of an octave between 'her' and 'arms', the tenor still maintains both the verbal and melodic cohesion of the phrase as a whole.

In public, McCormack sang in five languages; on record in four. He had tried Irish occasionally – as late as his first years in America – but he was not happy with the results. German Lieder (which he sang first in translation) became an essential part of his repertoire in the twenties. Unlike his Italian, McCormack did not have the opportunity to learn his German at first hand from native speakers, but depended upon his accompanist Teddy Schneider, Chicago-born but of German extraction, to coach him as they went on tour and on vacation. It did not prevent the tenor scoring a series of notable triumphs in Middle Europe, taking in Berlin in 1923; even if there were those who agreed with Herman Klein: 'I don't greatly admire his German accent, because it has an American flavour.' The accent apart, what is striking about McCormack's assumption of German Lieder is the genuineness of the emotions expressed in widely differing subjects. The mood of dejection with which he opens Schubert's 'Die Liebe hat gelogen', and which turns to anguish on 'Laß ab, mein Herz, zu klopfen', is in strong contrast to the almost whimsical happiness in remembrance of things past in Richard Strauss' 'Allerseelen'; while in Brahms' 'In Waldeseinsamkeit' he evokes something else again, with the ecstatic echoes of 'Ferne, ferne, ferne' in the final verse, and the fading pianissimo at the end of the last line: 'Sang ein Nachtigall'. Rarely does McCormack overreach himself. He knew his emotional and physical resources, and he knew how to match them.

Surprisingly, perhaps, his first Wolf recording, 'Wo find 'ich Trost' (1924) was not successful. Klein, when reviewing this record for the *Gramophone* in May 1927 thought of Schlusnus. 'What a blessing it would be if he could lend a little of his dark timbre to John McCormack! The rendering of our Irish tenor of "Wo find 'ich Trost" might then possess real significance, in addition to a sweet voice and a fluent method.'

Tone colour has much to do with taste, and almost as much to do with fashion. I suspect that today, having moved further away from romanticism, we require less expansiveness in style and vocal gesture, and therefore put a lower premium on darker, heavier voices than did Klein's generation. That said, it must be added that the tessitura of this song prevents McCormack's voice from sounding comfortable, or right for it. This record contains one of the few instances where the top register does not seem fully to belong to the rest of the voice. The quality is wrong: it is almost shrill. The text might justify that, but it does not evoke as much sympathy from the listener for he who is comfortless as a less pressing tonal quality might have done. In the twenties, McCormack recorded only one other song by Wolf: 'Schlafendes Jesuskind', which he was to repeat twice for the gramophone. In 1930 he made a rather austere version of 'Anacreon's Grab' without, at all, providing his usual charm. It is not until the mid-thirties that we get any idea of the affinity the tenor had for Wolf. His German repertoire extended to Wagner. A recording in English of 'The Prize Song' from *Die Meistersinger* (1916) is masterful. Even in the upper register the tenor sings well within his vocal powers and the voice remains beautifully poised. An ambition to sing the role of Walther remained unfulfilled.

In 1925, electrical recording was introduced. McCormack had brought the art of making the old acoustic horn work for him to a fine degree. He now discovered that his dynamic variations were translated to disc rather differently by the microphone and studio technician. On at least one occasion the tenor was provoked into asking who was making the record: he or the technician. Such difficulties were probably short lived; but what may have continued was the 'edge' the electrical process is said to have given to his voice. McCormack often described the acoustic process of recording as having been 'kinder' to his voice, and one can understand what he meant. The filtering of harmonics by the early process tended to make the voice sound smoother, and possibly warmer, than it may have sounded in live performance. There is a similar smoothness in the legato singing of Fernando de Lucia, Alessandro Bonci, Giuseppe Anselmi and Enrico Caruso, as well as many lesser lights of the acoustic age of recording. It seems unlikely that it could be wholly accounted for on the grounds of superior technique or a more ingratiating style. It is difficult to compare like with like: voices and age alter continually. But certainly Kreisler's violin tone, which was presumably less susceptible to change than the human voice, does sound warmer and smoother on acoustic disc.

In any case, I do not suppose that any record lover accepts what he hears on face value. Consciously and unconsciously he carries out a filtering process of his own, building up a mental image of a voice from the available material. In McCormack's case, we know just how exquisitely pure the voice must have been from such forward recordings as 'Parigi O Cara' and 'Come My Beloved', and one can impose to some extent the vocal colour from these records upon those which appear less satisfactory. So often among McCormack's Odeons, for example, the voice comes across as almost baritonal. But references to records made during the First World War – 'O Soave Fanciulla' from *La Bohème*, for instance, or 'Somewhere a Voice is Calling' – reveal just how light and delicate a tone McCormack must then have been producing. In one particular respect the gramophone leaves us in no doubt: the tenor's style of singing shows a gradual change of emphasis in the inherent tension that exists between the melodic and verbal demands of vocal music. The verbal takes an increasing precedence over the melodic. This is, as one would expect, especially evident after the middle thirties, when security in floating a vocal line can no longer be taken for granted.

It is interesting to find how differently reviewers could react to the increasing emphasis McCormack was placing on language. Herman Klein, for example, in discussing his recording of César Franck's 'Panis Angelicus', recorded in 1927, found it 'needless to add [that] the smooth quality of the voice is extremely ingratiating'. Latin is not a notably more mellifluous language than English, but in comparison with Klein, C. M. Crabtree found that with 'The Holy Child' and 'Just for Today' (both recorded in 1926):

> His one fault is surely that in singing in English he is seldom really smooth; he makes far too much of the characteristic English conjunction of final and initial consonants.

A more emphatic enunciation of final consonants than in the two records reviewed is to be found in 'Hymn to Christ the King', recorded in 1932. In the repetitions of the words 'Christ the King' the vowels are not lengthened at all, and so the consonants become very conspicuous. On this record McCormack's voice sounds out of condition, and the emphasis on the consonants was, I suspect, the result of this. But is it necessarily a fault? The question as to how much emphasis should be

Portrait of Fritz Kreisler, inscribed John Mac Cormack from his devo Fritz Kreisler.' An early tour the violinist made together failed finan McCormack wrote: 'The kindly the criticism which I received from those few concerts had a greater influe work than any other thing before or s

'Hymn to Christ the King'. Compos Vincent O'Brien, the hymn was rec by McCormack on 27 May 1932. I issued as a single-sided disc in aid o building fund of Liverpool Cathedral the obverse side of the disc was a pictu the Archbishop of Liverpool McCormack's favourite portrait of hi

placed on consonants is an old chestnut. And even if one were to accept that McCormack did make too much use of consonants on certain occasions, I do not think that the charge of lack of smoothness can be made against him. Even in his last records – in Mozart's 'To Chloë', for example, made during the tenor's very last recording session in September 1942, when the quality of the voice and intonation had become uncertain – the sense of line is so strong that the relationship between words and melody does not seem to be an unjust one. Compare 'Ah, Moon of My Delight' (1912) from *In a Persian Garden* with the aria from *The Mount of Olives* (1930). The earlier record reveals an ingratiating, nay, a ravishing legato and the words are less important. *The Mount of Olives* with its dramatic content is given, and can take, a greater verbal emphasis. But the vocalism remains extremely smooth, nonetheless. Neither record would be what it is had McCormack reversed their recording dates, which points to the importance of chronology in recording.

If his span of repertoire places McCormack apart, so too did the honours he received. They included a doctorate of literature conferred by Holy Cross, Massachusetts in 1917, and a doctorate of music from the National University of Ireland, conferred in 1927, rare recognitions for a performer. But it was his staunch, if hardly ascetic, commitment to the Roman Catholic Church and to her charities that brought the tenor his highest honour. In 1928 he was raised to the Papal peerage, an honour all

CLIMAX TO THE   GREAT CONGRESS

THE HIGH ALTAR IN THE PHŒNIX PARK.

OVER A MILLION PEOPLE AT MASS IN PHŒNIX PAR

McCormack as a canopy bearer in procession to Phœnix Park, Dublin the Pontifical High Mass in 1932.

the more unusual for being made hereditary. And it was as a Papal Count that McCormack had, perhaps, his finest hour, and certainly his largest live audience.

In 1932 the Eucharistic Congress was held in Dublin. The closing ceremonies and Pontifical High Mass took place in Phoenix Park, a few miles from the city centre. 'It was a day of a century', commented *The Irish Times*. That may have been an understatement. Estimates of the attendance in the park were put at one million; the population of the entire island was then less than four million. Led by the Papal Legate, Cardinal Lauri, a procession of cardinals, bishops, priests, dignitaries of state and the faithful left the city centre and made the journey to the park. There, on the steps of the high altar, resplendent in Papal uniform, McCormack sang Franck's 'Panis Angelicus', with a choir of five hundred. The service and song were broadcast live on radio and into the streets of Dublin direct by loudspeaker. Pathé News, from afar, photographed the tenor as he sang. The distance makes him appear no more than a tiny figure amongst scores of others. But the sound track is of considerable interest in offering us a documentary record of how the tenor sang to such a vast gathering. The phrasing, as always, is clearly defined and without ambiguity. A difficulty on this occasion, which would not have presented itself at any concert, was the confusion caused by the time lapse of the voice as it was broadcast through the local loudspeakers. Yet McCormack's vocal mien remains poised, and combines the illusion of expansiveness and intimacy.

A more tangible visual record of how the tenor appeared in person was made in 1929. This was the Fox film *Song O' My Heart*. Sound recording on film brought a spate of musical pictures following Al Jolson's *The Singing Fool* of 1927. *Song O' My Heart* was McCormack's only full-length feature film, but it meant that by 1930 he had made his presence felt in all the media of his time. Financially, it was a notably rewarding venture for him: eight weeks work earned him $500,000. The critic of *The Times* of 28 May 1930 was well aware of the difficulties inherent in making this kind of film: 'The sound film which is specially made as a background to a famous singer's voice generally has to yield dangerous measure in story value, or fail to do justice to its vocal possibilities.' A modern audience, with an interest in the singer or the songs, would probably agree with the same critic's conclusion that: 'The general impression of *Song O' My Heart* is that it was worth suffering the mawkishness of the story to hear Mr McCormack in his many enchanting moods.' And there is nothing mawkish about the unbroken concert sequence near the end of the film. It is to the eternal credit of the director, Frank Borzage, that he did not intersperse it with

'Tell me a story', a scene from the Song O' My Heart. This parti[cular] scene was shot in the grounds of M[...] Abbey.

the usual tearful or weeping lovers. The fact that the sequence is unbroken probably makes it unique in the history of film-making. And it brings us closer to the essential McCormack than any other record left to us. The stance, the head thrown back or slightly to one side, the closed eyes, all create an impression of extraordinary commitment to the music. There is a fervour, a dramatic impetus, even a virility that one might hardly suspect in listening to the studio recordings of Donaudy's 'Luoghi sereni e cari' or 'Ireland, Mother Ireland'.

After 1930, although the tenor was then only forty-six, and especially after 1932, the voice went into swift decline. *The Times* commented more than once in this period of a monotony in his tonal colour. This was almost certainly due to the demands involved in projecting the voice into an auditorium as large as the Albert Hall. However, it is difficult to think of a singer who used his declining resources on record with greater freshness, and the thirties contain some of his finest recordings. Most notable is the record he made of Wolf's 'Ganymed' in 1932, of which the music critic of the *Sunday Times*, Desmond Shawe-Taylor, has written:

He does supreme justice to one of the greatest of all German songs.
It is somewhat mysterious that McCormack seldom (if ever) sang

ABOVE *Moore Abbey, at Monasterevin, Co. Kildare, as it was when McCormack lived there in the 1930s.* LEFT *The drawing room.*

in public a song of which his interpretation is so memorable, indeed haunting, as to seem definitive. This is one of those rare performances which may properly be called inspired. A gentle pulsation enters the voice at the new access of emotion on the words 'Du kühlst den brennenden Durst meines Busens, lieblicher Morgenwind!', a wondering assent at 'Ich komme! ich komme!', a rapturous excitement at the phrase 'Mir! Mir! in eurem Schoße aufwarts!' while the long final phrase floats upward and out of sight, from the oft-repeated D to the high F sharp, in a manner of which this singer alone held the secret.

In 1935 McCormack recorded Wolf's 'Auch Kleine Dinge' with a mellowness, and 'Herr, Was Trägt der Boden Hier' with an incisive poignancy that he could hardly have evoked earlier. It was with these two songs that Elena Gerhardt chose to open her Wolf Society Album, and in October 1940 the *Gramophone* aptly noted in reference to McCormack's 'Herr, Was Trägt der Boden Hier':

It moves one in rather a different way to Gerhardt's recording. It is the cry of a broken man rather than that of one still in the full vigour of life. . . .

McCormack and his manager, Dennis F. McSweeney. McCormack relied heavily upon those who travelled with him for companionship. McSweeney had been a boon companion to him for twenty years, up till his death in 1934 – shortly after this picture was taken. McCormack then seemed to lose some of his old zest for the concert circuit.

Singing tends to be the prerogative of youth. Age, if it offers a compensation, does so in contributing experience of life. Youth can only look forward. Age can look back. This dimension served McCormack well in many of the items he recorded when he was past fifty. His ballads now offered reflectiveness and touches not likely to be met with in a younger man. The whimsical quality that the tenor imparts to the two Foster songs, 'Jeannie with the Light Brown Hair' and 'Sweetly She Sleeps, My Alice Fair', could only belong to his maturity. In 'The Garden Where the Praties Grow' the hint of a chuckle on the line:

...the role of Papal Chamberlain. His ...es included ushering in visitors for ...ences with His Holiness. The picture ...scribed: 'God bless the "Capuchin ...nual" yours sincerely John Count ...Cormack, Sept. 7th 1936.'

'Two boys just like their mother *and the girl's the image of me*' is surely the effect of a man who has known parenthood and can look back upon it. The 1934 Victor recording of 'Terence's farewell to Kathleen' is an altogether more effective version than the Odeon one, made twenty-seven years earlier. Then the story was understood rather than felt, stated rather than unfolded. On the Victor record, Terence's predicament is personalized and becomes a drama enacted out in this life times without number.

A rare failure is to be found in 'The Kerry Dance' (1936), which is

137

much less evocative of times past than the earlier version in 1916. The tenor appears unequal to the demands of sustaining the line through the awkward divisions in this song. One might be tempted to conclude from this record that the voice had gone too far by this date, were there not superlatively communicative things to come. Only the month after 'The Kerry Dance' came his last recording of 'Schlafendes Jesuskind' where, in subdued mood, McCormack seeks out the mystery of religious imagery. Piano accompaniment, during these years, suited the tenor better than orchestral accompaniment. And in 'The Old House', specially written by General Sir Frederick O'Connor for his farewell performances, with the crystalline piano accompaniment, or collaboration, of Gerald Moore, we hear McCormack provide inimitable poignancy to simple lines:

> Lone is the house now, and lonely the moorland,
> The children are scattered, the old folk are gone,
> Why stand I here like a ghost and a shadow,
> 'Tis time I was moving, 'tis time I passed on.

On 17 March 1937, at Buffalo, the tenor left the American recital circuit with, as the *New York Times* put it, 'a gay wave of his hand and a soft good-bye, drowned in thunderous applause'. But the following year, on 27 November 1938, it was a tearful farewell that he bade to a packed Albert Hall in London. Retirement rested heavily on the tenor's shoulders. A trip to Cairo followed by a fishing holiday in Ireland left the tenor restless. A singer finds it hard to admit that the race has been run; and with the outbreak of the Second World War McCormack toured the British Isles, assisted by the baritone Robert Irwin and the·

The tenor entertaining F. J. McCorm and other members of the Abbey The Company at a party given in Hollywoo the spring of 1938. The Abbey Comp was on a tour of the States.

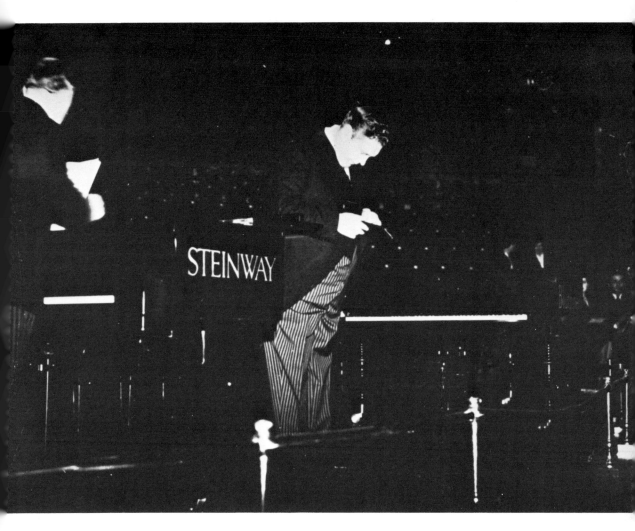

The tenor takes a bow during his farewell at the Albert Hall, 27 November 1938. 'John McCormack's like we shall certainly not hear again. In Handel's "Where'er you Walk" we were given a lesson in the rounding of Italianate phrases, while in two of the smaller and quieter Wolf songs he once more achieved a miracle in showing them to us exactly as they are even in the circus maximus that is the Albert Hall.' (Ernest Newman in the Sunday Times, 4 December 1938)

RIGHT The Count in retirement, fishing on the R. Slaney in Ireland.

Thanks for your letter
your [illegible]
John Count de [illegible]
1942

A VERY PEACEFUL CHRISTMAS AND VICTORIOUS NEW YEAR

'Glena', Booterstown, Co. Dublin, where the tenor died on 16 September 1945.

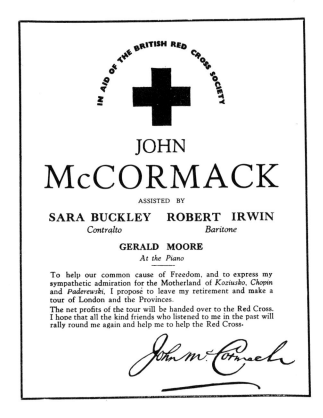

IN AID OF THE BRITISH RED CROSS SOCIETY

JOHN
McCORMACK

ASSISTED BY

SARA BUCKLEY **ROBERT IRWIN**
Contralto *Baritone*

GERALD MOORE
At the Piano

To help our common cause of Freedom, and to express my sympathetic admiration for the Motherland of *Koziusko, Chopin* and *Paderewski*, I propose to leave my retirement and make a tour of London and the Provinces.
The net profits of the tour will be handed over to the Red Cross. I hope that all the kind friends who listened to me in the past will rally round me again and help me to help the Red Cross.

Programme for the final tour.

contralto Sarah Buckley, on behalf of the Red Cross. BBC broadcasts on the popular Irish Half Hour series followed. Recording sessions continued until 1942, when emphysema made further singing impossible. The tenor lived for eighteen months in the Shelbourne Hotel, Dublin, and then moved to 'Glena' in Booterstown, Co. Dublin, where he died on 16 September 1945. He was sixty-one.

If it is true that as a recitalist McCormack had no real predecessor, it is equally true that he has had no real successor. As Henry Pleasants remarks in *Serious Music and All That Jazz*:

> Some can remember when John McCormack, Caruso, Schumann-Heink, Kreisler, Cortot, Rachmaninov, and Tauber performed, in their recitals and on records, music, sometimes of their own composition, that is regarded today as beneath the dignity of a Serious musician. This was still true of such younger artists as John Charles Thomas, Richard Crooks, Lawrence Tibbett and Ezio Pinza; but they all lived to see it rather counted against them. Furthermore, what they thought of as popular music was no longer so popular.

This, in fact, was also true for McCormack towards the end of his career; and he knew it. Quoting from an interview given by the tenor after his final appearance in Boston in 1936, *The Boston Post* of February 1944 recalled:

> To shake him from his feeling of sadness he was told he had many friends in Boston. 'That isn't so at all', he exploded. 'Nobody in Boston cares about me any more. I'm too old. My day is over. The public is interested in younger men.'

Some overstatement aside, what McCormack said was fundamentally true. The vast audiences in America who had responded to him with such acclaim in the twenties were no longer so large or so enthusiastic. It was not, however, to a younger man in an even vaguely similar vocal tradition that the baton had been handed. By way of comparison, *The Boston Post* thought of Frank Sinatra as the up and coming youngster most likely to emulate the tenor's successes.

The paper might also have quoted Bing Crosby, for it was with the Old Groaner that the era of the microphone singer arrived. In 1926 Crosby recorded his first disc and his first million-seller came ten years

...lies in concentration and relaxation. ...left the tenor broadcasts for NBC. On ... the young Crosby shares a song with ...nk Sinatra. Singing now meant ...ething different.

later. The vocal revolution which was in the making was neatly illustrated by the fact that whereas McCormack had been sensitive to singing much popular material, the opposite now worked for Crosby. 'Jack Kapp (a recording manager with Brunswick) had much trouble talking me into recording 'Adeste, Fideles',' Crosby confessed, 'being only a crooner, I felt that I didn't have sufficient stature as a singer to sing a song with religious implications.' But his very lack of stature was to Crosby's advantage and no one knew that better than Crosby himself. As he wrote in his autobiography, *Going My Way*:

> I think – and I'm confident that my assumption is correct – that every man who . . . listens to one of my records or who hears me on the radio believes firmly that he sings as well as I do, especially when he's in the bathroom shower. It's no trick for him to believe this, because I have none of the mannerisms of a trained singer and I have very little voice. If I've achieved any success as a warbler it's because I've managed to keep the kind of naturalness in my style, my phrasing and my mannerisms which any Joe Doakes possesses.
>
> They feel no kinship for a wonderful register and an elaborate range. They realize that he's achieved something they can never

McCormack's Mass Appeal Was Greater Than Crooners'

Cartoon from the Boston Sunday Post, *February 1944 (McCormack is portrayed as Tonio from* La Fille du Regiment). *That a newspaper should have chosen to compare a non-microphone or what could then have been described as an orthodox singer with a microphone one is, in itself, an interesting sidelight on musical and social history.*

hope to achieve. But it's my hunch that most men feel that if th had gotten the opportunity I've had, they could have done just well.

No opera singer could have written that. Nor could McCorm However deceptive the ease with which the tenor sang 'Il Tesoro' or 'Mother Machree', no Joe Doakes was likely to imagin could do the same. McCormack had made the art of singing i accessible, more tangible through the recital format and thro expanding his repertoire. He did not alter the art itself. The microph did. It produced a new kind of vocalism on an altogether more intin often homespun, plane. By contrast, the whole genus of 'operatic non-microphone singing began to appear as aloof and distant, and artificial. Very quickly the respective repertoires for the two kind singing divided along the now familiar lines of 'serious' and 'popu. There are alternative terms. 'Serious' music tends to correspond clo to period music, 'popular' to contemporary music. The term 'per singer, however, is never used as an alternative to 'serious'. The reaso all too clear. It would give implicit recognition to the fact that 'serious' singer has now little contemporary relevance.

But that fact is too important to be overlooked. It has changed function of the 'serious' singer. McCormack's career and style, it see to me, represent a watershed between the role of the 'serious' singer as found it when he began his career, and what it has become since. 'serious' singer since McCormack has been truly contemporary with society in which he lives. He has little contemporary music to manif. He has become, instead, a guardian of the past. This has altered relationship that used to obtain between the 'serious' singer and audience. The onus of guardianship has changed the performer of into the modern presenter. The change is manifest on record.

Philadelphia Inquirer *cartoon, 29 October 1961. One of the best-known stories in early-century opera lore is how McCormack greeted Caruso with: 'And how is the world's greatest tenor?' To which Caruso replied: 'And since when have you become a baritone?' A generation after McCormack's death the story was still current, as this cartoon shows.*

PERFORMER
VERSUS PRESENTER

> The development of consciousness in human beings is inseparably
> connected with the use of metaphor. Metaphors are not merely
> peripheral decorations or even useful models, they are fundamental
> forms of our awareness.
> Irish Murdoch: *The Sovereignty of the Good*

In a television interview, the American baritone Sherill Milnes wryly
informed the interviewer that when he wants to interpolate a high note,
he 'asks permission' from the conductor. Times change. While
preparing for a performance of Verdi's *Macbeth* to be staged in Dublin in
1859, the conductor, Luigi Arditi, was pleased to receive a letter from
the mezzo-soprano Pauline Viardot which began: 'Dear Maestro, Here
are the transpositions which I am making in the part of Lady Macbeth.
. . .' Neither the example of Reeves and his whistling wife quoted in
Chapter 1 nor that of Viardot, who was an authoritative musician as well
as a singer, is probably quite typical of the age in which it occurred,
but I should think they are indicative of the status and autonomy that a
singer might then expect as his or her birthright; and whose resulting
approach and style of singing the acoustic gramophone documented at
the time of its inception.

According to today's precepts, such autonomy for the singer is neither
necessary nor desirable. It is not necessary, because the function of the
singer is to reproduce faithfully the score as written. And it is undesirable
because it is the paternal or autocratic adjudication of the conductor that
offers the best safeguard against that function being exceeded. Ironically,
the age of the acoustic gramophone can furnish evidence in support of
these precepts as well as against them. For what operated previously, as
J. B. Steane has written in his book *The Grand Tradition*, was:

a perilous system. . . . Nowadays our musical expectations are both more secure and more narrow; we have no reason to fear performances so bad that a composer would not know his own music, yet we have almost as little hope for any so good that will stay in the mind as something irreplaceably individual and marvellous.

There is probably enough evidence of bad taste from the period, at least by today's reckoning, to make a case for contending that if the age was not actually a decadent one, it was one in which decadence was rife.

There are probably many who agree with Henry Pleasants when he wrote in *The Great Singers from the dawn of opera to our own time* that today 'The level of competence is high – possibly higher than ever – but its effectiveness is compromised by uniformity', and many who would prefer things that way. Not so the author, who in *Serious Music and All That Jazz* puts forward his view of present-day singing unequivocally:

> The performer in Serious music . . . is expected to play the notes, all the notes and nothing but the notes; and he is expected to play them exactly as written. Critics and many lay listeners follow his performance in the concert hall or on the phonograph record in the living room, score in hand, holding him accountable for every dot and double dot. . . . That some performers still achieve distinction despite the appallingly narrow range of options speaks for their ingenuity, as does their proud rationalization of this pedantry as 'fidelity to the score'.

By comparison, Max de Schauensee is content to end his British Institute of Recorded Sound lecture, 'Emma Eames and other singers I have known', with this comment:

> I do not think that at any particular time standards have been greater or better: what they have been is *different*. Fashions change in food, dress, manners and everything else, including opera.

Different standards; of that there can be no doubt. The acoustic gramophone has provided incontrovertible evidence that singing meant something different at the turn of the century than it does today. However, a comparison of standards, like a comparison of morals, tends to be inconclusive because one is necessarily talking about just that: different standards. A more useful approach, it seems to me, is to ask this question: granted that the 'acoustic' singers sang differently, is there any way in which that difference can be described?

I believe it can, with the proviso added that sports are apparent in any age. Just as philosophers like to designate the seventeenth century as the Age of Reason, and it is not difficult to find unreasoning men in it, so it is not difficult to find singers who defy the general bent. The object of the exercise is to try and define that bent. We may reasonably presume, as a starting point, that the Victorian singer, and to some extent the Edwardian singer also, was not expected to sing and did not sing 'all the notes and nothing but the notes', nor all the notes as written. Was this merely a matter of individual whim? Or can some underlying approach be determined?

Despite the individuality of the early gramophone singers, there is a remarkable unity about their style of singing and the alterations and departures from the score that they made. These can be shown to repeat themselves time and again throughout the era of acoustic recording, with much greater frequency than in modern years and probably with declining frequency if one views the span of recording as a whole. The early singers' style appears to stem from an attitude to singing quite removed from our own. No one is likely to quarrel with the description of music as a mode or type of communication. But whereas present thinking seems to assume that all, or almost all, the elements of communication are to be found in the composition and the singer has no more to do than *present* the score, the Victorian view seems to have been that the very act of performing is itself inherent to the process of communication.

What then was the Victorian and Edwardian singer doing, that we meet with less frequency today? He was, I believe, constantly creating and sustaining a *linear tension* over and above the tensions and releases native to all melodic music. This can be illustrated in numerous ways. And nowhere more strikingly than in the Victorian use of pauses which often came where one would least expect them today. Take for example, Olimpia Boronat's recording of 'Qui la Voce' from Bellini's *I Puritani*, which was recorded in 1904. J. B. Steane, in discussing this record in *The Grand Tradition*, includes these remarks:

> . . . *is* this 'the true way to sing Bellini', or, more specifically, to sing this aria? With a big breath in the first phrase, and another in the second? . . . And did Bellini really want the verb and its object, let alone the notes of his phrase, put asunder by the 'lunga pausa' (for breath) that we hear in 'ah, rendetemi la speme'?

Breath the singer certainly takes in the phrases mentioned, but it is a mistake, I think, to regard them as pauses made for the purpose of taking breath. Rather, they are pauses which are inserted to heighten the melodic tension and in which breath is taken. The long phrase held no fear for Boronat, as witness how she ends the aria with a long-drawn diminuendo on 'morir'. Such pregnant breaks as these, in mid-stream, were a feature of Boronat's singing; and, more important, they were wholly characteristic of the age. One finds it in the art of those who are taken to represent that age: Mattia Battistini, Adelina Patti, Marcella Sembrich, and Fernando de Lucia of whom Steane notes that he:

> sometimes takes a breath that modern singers would try to avoid. Yet paradoxically the flow of his singing is a feature that memory retains as one of his most remarkable characteristics.

Silence, no less than sound, was exploited by the Victorian singer as a potent source of linear tension. Thus, on acoustic disc, one rarely finds the singer lapsing into quietude. He pauses only, and constantly nurtures our sense of expectancy for the rest of the phrase or the next phrase to follow.

Such pauses are created, they do not just happen, and the singer employed one or more of several devices to create them. Familiar to us still is the practice of clipping short the time value of the final note of the phrase and thereby enhancing the need for resolution or continuation. Less common today, perhaps, is the upward, sometimes microtonal, inflexion on the last note of a phrase. The opera singers of the acoustic age reveal that once upon a time this device was not the sole property of the jazz musician. Giuseppe Anselmi offers vivid examples of this in 'Una Vergine' from *La Favorita*, but instances abound.

More numerous still and used with decidedly more purposefulness than today are examples of the art of slowing down, extending a phrase as it draws to a close; or, conversely, contracting it, hurrying it up. Both practices equally created a sense of a brink at the end of a phrase. And this leads to the central feature of the performer's art. The composer may apply, as general directions, the terms *accelerando* and *ritardando* to passages and even phrases. What he cannot do is prescribe them for the precise manipulations of every part of every phrase. Such manipulations are too short, too subtle and too frequent for the written score. And it was with this discretionary faculty, above all others, for urging forward in a phrase and pulling back, that the singer attained a linear tension that goes beyond what can be notated. He slowed down and savoured with his audience what he found most appealing, and passed over more quickly what he regarded as less important. *He was, in effect, providing a commentary upon his material.* This was therefore, essentially, a performer's art.

It was also an optional art, since dispensed with by the 'serious' musician in favour of literal presentations of the score. The singer now fulfils a function similar to that of the earliest ciné photographers, in

The Neapolitan tenor Fernando de (1860–1925). McCormack first he Lucia around 1906 in Milan in Barber of Seville. 'We often wen café in the Galleria, where the young a and students paraded every afternoon . watch "The Great Ones" walking or sitting outside cafes drinking aper Lily recalled in I Hear You Ca Me. 'Once, with almost bated breath, told me that I was looking at Fernan Lucia, an idolized tenor of the day u silver voice and superb acting John ad extravagantly.'

taking up a fixed and neutral position in relation to his subject. He is diametrically opposed to the modern photographer, in whose hands the motion of the camera has become a form of commentary in its own right. The modern singer does not offer a linear motion above what is to be found in the score: the score must speak for itself. So the performer of old has given place to the modern presenter. Not, however, in jazz, where the performer's art remains obligatory. Not for nothing is it a commonplace of jazz jargon, as Henry Pleasants has noted in *Serious Music and All That Jazz*, 'that a musician who is thought to swing is considered a jazzman, and that one who does not is not.' And swinging is incompatible with a literal presentation of the score, indeed they are impossible to combine. For 'swinging' is maintained by nothing other than 'rhythmic pulsations and . . . tensions resulting from controlled rhythmic deviation'. There is, therefore, a startling similarity between the jazz musician and the Victorian opera singer. But whereas the jazz musician can obtain his melodic flight or 'swing' only by offsetting his melodic line against the vital and explicit beat of his music, the opera singer or singer of European music does not have an equal dependence upon, or support from, the implicit beat contained in his music. He could, without compromising his linear and rhythmic tension, choose to discount the beat in the written score.

Some did, and none more so than the Neapolitan tenor Fernando de Lucia. He made of the implicit beat something remote and even indeterminate, so that the rhythmic pulse, as scored, should have no claim over the tensions of his own extensive line. It made his art unique. And for that very reason it was, probably even in his own time, a parochial art, best understood and so carried to its furthest limits amongst those most familiar with the tenor's ways – the audiences of his native city, Naples. One may be certain that they made no comparison of their hero with the written score, nor heard with bemused ears an interminable unravelling of laboured phrases as modern ears are wont to do. No, de Lucia transformed his audiences' ears into eyes; and, thus transformed, they followed his melodic line as if it had a graphic shape and a graphic motion. Then the tenor would suspend the movement of the phrase and hold it, before their eyes, as if in mid-air, as if motionless. A rapt audience might dare the linear tension to break and the phrase to fall to earth. But de Lucia's judgement rarely faltered. His melodic line, through sound and silence, remained a thing of perfection.

No wonder J. B. Steane can remark of the age: 'Accomplishment in florid music and the cultivation of a true legato seem to have been the dominant technical interests.' Embellishment served the performer by enabling him to introduce additional tensions and releases within the flow of the melodic line. A marvellous example of an embellishment used for that purpose is the turn de Lucia introduces on the B flat in the rising phrase: 'Sorriso dell' amor' from the aria 'De' Miei Bollenti Spiriti' from *La Traviata*. He pirouettes on the spot when we expect him to continue his ascent upwards, and then, with the subtlest emphasis, draws our attention to the fact that he is already within one note of the crest. A true legato is, of course, essential to instrumental singing, but it is not quite the basis of the performer's art. Linear tension is, after all, as much the result of a mental as a physical progression and can be manifest in staccato as much as in legato singing. In technical accomplishment and its application, the gramophone suggests de Lucia was the extremity in an age of performers. As the age moved on, the performer's art drew closer to and less conspicuous beside the composer's score. The progression continued until the composer's score, apparently, eclipsed the performer's art and deviation from the score came to mean infidelity to the score.

In the process a critical fact has been lost to sight, namely, that *deviation from the score* and the *performer's art* are not interchangeable terms. Deviation, of itself, does not necessarily yield linear tension, nor is compliance with the melodic tensions and releases in the score necessarily incompatible with it. Moreover, no score is ever rendered in exactly the same way by any two singers, for musical notation is not an exact system in the way that mathematics is. The relationship between the performer's art and deviation is far from being a direct one. What distinguishes the Victorian singers from the moderns is not the greater extent to which they deviated from the score. It is the greater extent to which they made use of deviation.

It is this which entitles the early gramophone singers to be called performers, and John McCormack may be included in their number. Wholly characteristic of his discography is his use of this art of creating a perpetual sense of expectancy and revelation, of inexhaustible momentum. Compared with his contemporaries McCormack used the performer's licence with restraint, even austerity, especially in his operatic repertoire: a feature remarkable for being found in some of his most spontaneous singing on record. Ostensibly, his close observance of the score would seem to place him at a fair remove from the libertarian and cavalier Victorians and Edwardians, for instance Alessandro Bonci and Giuseppe Anselmi, with whose lyrical gifts McCormack's are often compared. McCormack's use of *rubato* was in sharp contrast to theirs: he interpreted the term as 'borrowed time', and whatever rhythmic variations he employed he almost invariably maintained the same duration of the song or aria. The two Italians, typically of the

period, thought of *rubato* as 'stolen time'. They were not unduly concerned with paying back. Yet I doubt if McCormack's style and approach to singing could have developed in any other context than in this period of transition between the Victorian vocal attitudes and the modern ones.

McCormack brought to his art an innate discipline, wholly his own, and thereby *integrated* the dual claims of the composer's score and his own needs as a performer in a manner possibly not equalled before, and with the dissolution of the performer's art probably not possible to achieve again. Nowhere is this integration more apparent than in his singing of Don Ottavio's aria 'Il Mio Tesoro' from *Don Giovanni*. The Victorians, with their predilection for working from the score rather than through it, provided Mozart with, as Desmond Shawe-Taylor has said of Battistini: 'a period flavour which could never, I believe, seem right again'. Yet it is what McCormack drew from the Victorians that, paradoxically, made his recording inimitable. The gramophone reveals that he drew two things: this linear tension and an 'instrumental' style of singing. Neither singly nor together could these elements be said to constitute McCormack's conception of the aria, but nor could his conception have been constituted without them. It was a conception of classically conceived balance. Balance between movements in opposition, for a vocal line entails the sense of movement on a vertical as well as a horizontal plane. McCormack manipulated his vocal line with a sense of movement that was quite unambiguous. The form he gave to this aria is now taken as the standard, even if no one has sung it since with quite the same shapeliness and precision. And after Richard Tauber one is not likely to find a comparable projection of linear tension or an equal security in instrumental singing.

A comparison so often made between an example of singing and the sound of a violin depends for its justification on the *build* of the voice. The essential feature of a bowed instrument is that the resonance of the scale tapers imperceptibly from the lowest to the highest notes. The listener will readily respond to this feature but he may not understand why. In conjunction with pitch, it enables him to sense the relative altitude of any note by its comparative resonance. The more perfect the taper of tonal resonance, the greater will be the definition of the phrase. The saying that the history of composition is the history of the infraction of the rule has a useful parallel here in singing. The disproportionate girth of resonance that Caruso gave to his top notes was an infraction of instrumental singing and an exhilarating one it was. But no tenor subsequent to McCormack has been able to divest himself entirely of that infraction. Caruso and the Verismo tradition divided the past from present. Even

...e Italian tenor Alessandro Bonci ...870–1940). Of all the operatic tenors to ...ear in America, Bonci was the only one ...any way to rival Caruso. Bonci and ...rnando de Lucia are sometimes thought of ...representing a school of lyricism more ...ical of the early than the late nineteenth, ...twentieth, century. Bonci's records, ...wever, are something of an enigma. One ...led to believe that effortless singing was a ...e qua non of those who first essayed ...ellini and Donizetti. Bonci's singing is ...idly, often exquisitely lyrical, but ...fortless? Not on record at any rate. It is ...orth bearing this in mind when noting that ...IcCormack – who would have heard ...onci and de Lucia many times in the flesh ...greatly preferred de Lucia.

153

Tauber used a very Carusoesque top frequently; and for all his mere-thread-of-sound effects, perhaps from an inherent weakness at the top, could never quite do without some measure of that infraction.

Perhaps only one other tenor besides McCormack had the absolute facility for rising on the scale with perfect diminution of resonance. As one listens to him swerving first to left and then to right of the score, until 'Il Mio Tesoro' sounds misshapen, it is ironic to think that de Lucia alone might have rivalled McCormack's performance; but Victorian romanticism would not allow him to return to classical shapes. McCormack made the journey instead, and for this century was Mozart's most zealous 'apostle of proportion'.

It was not, however, in Mozart or in opera that McCormack revealed the fullest breadth of the performer's art, but in songs in English. For it was the English language that provided him with his primary vehicle for rhythmic deviation. Outside the microphone genre of singers, his relationship with the language was probably unique. The aural comprehension of speech depends largely upon the speaker's employing its stresses and accents as in common usage. But for speech to be regarded as natural, the degree of latitude by which such stresses and accents may vary is critically defined by the ear. McCormack was uncompromising in remaining within that latitude. The rhythms of speech and music are in constant conflict. It was to those of speech that McCormack gave priority. The result was that he sang the language as he might have spoken it, and his melodic line continually deviated rhythmically, while he yet maintained its essential shapes. It is difficult to think of another singer in whom verbal naturalness could be so consistently counted upon to prevail against the exigencies of vocal placement. All the more remarkable, therefore, that McCormack did not use such facility *pour épater la bourgeoisie*. We have that on no less an authority than Ernest Newman, who wrote: 'I never knew him in his public or private singing to be guilty of a lapse of taste.'

But virtue in a changing world is not always recognized for what it is. After a McCormack concert in the Albert Hall in 1932 the critic of *The Times* was raising his voice against 'loose rhythm and slack phrasing', while having no difficulty in admitting to the tenor's 'directness of statement . . . that will reach where a more conscious art and a stricter craftsmanship will fail to penetrate'. What art, one may well ask, is 'more conscious' or what craftsmanship 'stricter' than that which offers 'directness of statement'? Was this not a sign that the day of the performer was being overtaken by that of the presenter? Perhaps it was inevitable that it should be.

One tends to think of McCormack as a comparatively modern tenor.

Modern in the sense that he sang up to and during the Second World War; modern also because a substantial part of his recording career overlapped the advent of electrical recording. But his roots lay with the Victorian performer, and it was contemporary popular music that made it possible to nurture those roots. His career encompassed a period when 'serious' and 'popular' music were not yet mutually exclusive, but had a relationship of tension. McCormack exploited that tension. He provided the classics with the immediacy he and his audience experienced with popular music. He gave to popular music the technique, the discipline and the musicianship he derived from the classics. In a manner not possible to equal since, he had synthesized the parts of a diverging repertoire. And this may go some way to explain what was his most pervasive virtue. For above the voice and the immaculate technique, and even when the voice was no longer young and vigorous, John McCormack remained, always, a vividly communicative artist. No closer definition of the function of the performer exists. And it was the vividness with which the tenor fulfilled this function that one feels intuitively belongs to an age that is done. But one does not have to rely on intuition: the gramophone is a ready witness.

PICTURE CREDITS

Boston Sunday Post: 144
Liam Breen: 59, 94
Cyril, Count McCormack: 118, 119
Edison Laboratory National Monument: 14, 19
Gramophone: 41
Illustrated London News: 16
John McCormack Society of Ireland: 79, 81, 100, 130, 138
King Features: 145
Library of Congress: 109
McCormack Association of Greater Kansas City: 90–1
McCormack Society of America: 106
National Library of Ireland: 34, 74, 75
New York Public Library: 150
Seamus O'Dwyer: 24, 32 (top left)
Punch: 64–5, 88
Royal Opera, Covent Garden: 56–7, 152
Radio Times Hulton Picture Library: 73 (left), 139 (top)
Sunday Times: 114
Talking Machine Review-International: 17, 21 (top), 33
The Times: 21 (below)
T. J. Walsh: 40
R. L. Webster: 36 (right), 78, 92, 125 (below)
R. D. Williams: 103

SELECTED BIBLIOGRAPHY

Dolan, P. Article in *The Sword of Light,* spring 1974. (Authoritative resumé on McCormack's North American career.)

Foxall, R., *John McCormack*. London, 1963.

Key, P., *John McCormack, his own life story*. Boston, 1918.

MacDermott Roe, L. F., *The John McCormack discography*. Surrey, 1972. (Various corrections and additions to this discography have been printed from time to time in the Newsletter of The John McCormack Society of America.)
Moore, G. *Am I too loud?* London, 1962.
McCormack, L., *I Hear You Calling Me*. London, 1950.
Strong, L. A. G., *John McCormack*. London, 1941.

Wagner, C. L., *Seeing Stars*. New York, 1940.

Scarry, J., 'Finnegan's Wake, A portrait of John McCormack', in *Irish University Review*, Vol. III, No. 2, Autumn 1973.

Letters.
John McCormack: correspondence with Charles L. Wagner. Heinman collection case, Library of Congress, Washington D.C.

INDEX